THE SCENE / 2
(Plays from Off-Off-Broadway)

Edited by
STANLEY NELSON

special report by TOM TOLNAY

THE SMITH / NEW EGYPT

NOTICE: All rights in the following plays are fully reserved and copyrighted. No performance, broadcast, public reading, recitation or presentation of any kind may be given without prior authorization of the authors and their agents. For information, contact New Egypt Publications, 5 Beekman Street, New York, N.Y. 10038.

© Copyright March 15, 1974 by The Smith. Volume II, complete. Published by The Smith under the New Egypt imprint, in association with The Generalist Association, 5 Beekman Street, New York, N.Y. 10038

Printed at Liberal Press, 80 Fourth Ave., New York, New York

Edited by Stanley Nelson

$3.50 per copy. The Scene, 5 Beekman Street, New York, N.Y. 10038

Library of Congress Catalog Card Number 72-89382. ISBNO-912292-34-2
Copyright © by The Scene. First printing, March, 1974

Distributed by Horizon Press, 156 Fifth Ave., N.Y., N.Y. 10010

Contents

	Page
A Business Of The Spirit Tom Tolnay	5
The Groups	11
We Hate to See You Go Michael McGrinder	19
Magic Time William Kushner	39
Family, Family Sally Ordway	48
Coffee Stand Sharon Thie	59
1 Piece Smash Arthur Sainer	81
Living Room With 6 Oppressions Oscar Mandel	85
Simultaneous Transmissions Robert Patrick	124
OOB Trends	130
One Act, Five Scenes	135
The Wrath of God (Act I) Joseph Renard	136
The Blasphemy of Rimbaud's Sister (scene) Robert Herron and Alexander Gotfryd	155

New York Transit Authority (scene)
Joseph Lazarus   161

The Women's Representative (scene)
Sun Yu   166

Mrs. Peacock (scene)
Stanley Nelson   175

Applejuice
Francine Trevens   180

222 Off-Off Broadway Theatres   184

Cover Design and Photo Layout: Al Ingegno
The Scene: Photoessay by Michael Campione: Pages 97-104

OFF-OFF-BROADWAY

A Business of the Spirit

TOM TOLNAY

Off-off Broadway theatre continues to grow, that much is certain. To what extent and in which direction it is expanding may be measured in a variety of ways, depending upon how the OOB stage—that indefinite & indefatigable creature—is presented.

In a strictly numerical accounting, for instance, the last edition of this book listed 117 theatres or groups in New York City. In this second tabulation we list 228 theatres or companies—helpless in the knowledge that we've missed others somewhere in the basement of a stolid apartment house, or damp-smelling, abandoned movie theatre, or drafty store front. They're out there all right, but where?

Granted, not all of the boost in this year's list is occasioned by theatres new to the scene. Some undoubtedly existed the last time around and were simply not caught up with until this printing. Others skipped a year or two before reappearing, mushroom-like, this past season. But most of that extra number are new manifestations of the theatre —a convincing argument for the vitality, the self-replenishing power of the movement. Especially since that total was achieved despite the fact that a considerable number of theatres also returned to dust during the past year.

The most dramatic example of that dustification occurred when in one roaring flop—which is exactly what happened to the feeble Broadway Central Hotel, it collapsed—six theatres were wiped off the scene and, thereby, our slate. The theatres were part of what was known as the Mercer Arts Complex. The Gene Frankel Acting Studio, home of many OOB productions, also went down in smoke.

Tom Tolnay is editor of BACKSTAGE.

We might also present the growth of off-off-Broadway by collecting the thousands of printed and broadcast reviews that have appeared over the past decade. Embodied in these varied personal accountings of individual examples of the phenomenon is a veritable anthological history of the movement, with the names and places and productions —and even some notion of their artistic development—recorded for, that's right, posterity.

Flipping through a batch of those many individual excursions into the OOB phantasmagoria would give a degree of motion and meaning to the many ideas and energies that make up OOB— rather like flipping those old cards that "moved" a cowpoke from one side of the card to the other. Such an overview of the movement would demonstrate, this writer believes, an increasing excitement surrounding what is being staged in the "suburbs" of Broadway. Perhaps "sub-orbs" would be more accurate, for it is decidely a world beneath the main stage. A sub-culture that is peculiar in that it has managed to exist, to grow no less, without reliance upon profit. And in this country, that makes it very curious indeed.

For what it's worth (and that's for you to decide) an increasing number of honors have leaked down into this sub-world. In fact, there's a prize-winning play in the collection assembled between these covers. "The Women's Representative," written by Sun Yu, won first prize in the People's Playwriting contest of Peking. First produced in New York at the Night House, the play was then presented in Puerto Rico as part of the World Theatrical Festival—ironically representing New York. "The Death of Solly's Warren" by Stuart Oderman, not included here, is another prize-winning play from OOB. Performed at the Omni Theatre Club, this one acquired honors in the Smith-Per/Se Awards. So OOB has taken its curtain calls, and one supposes that's as good a way as the next to show that it is an expanding force in the business of proferring ideas on stage.

Or one might declare that OOB is growing "by leaps and bounds," literally, for the movement includes a sizeable number of dance

SPECIAL REPORT 7

companies which, like the theatrical department of OOB, covers the full range of dance experience: modern, jazz, ballet, and an undeduced number of original dance viewpoints, some known well, others remote. Companies devoted strictly to dance have not been included in our list, but a fair guess would place their New York number at not much under 100. Some theatres on our list also present dance programs—the Cubiculo, for one.

Another way to characterize the growth, or at least range, of OOB would be to sing the praises of still another avenue of the trend —off-off-Broadway opera. With no accurate measure available (and little chance of being challenged) we estimate that at least 25 elbow-grease opera companies perform light or heavy-weight productions in and around New York City. Often these productions are in full regalia, lacking only real blood; others are merely stand-up performances, without prop or costume. In most, performers sing every note written. Because of the theatrical nature of these productions, and the endurance of the companies, several of the longer established opera units have been included in our tabulation.

The geographic form of OOB is changing, too. Greenwich Village used to be the center of OOB, the headquarters. And this is another way we might gauge its growth—horizontally instead of vertically. Petite theatres are showing up everywhere, in the most unlikely quarters of the city. What used to be a Village phenomenon has not only spread all over Manhattan—but across the East River to Brooklyn and Queens, even north over the Harlem River to the Bronx. Staten Island, too, is showing signs of donning the mask.

Another measure, one that is a uniquely American, to determine when an industry or institution has arrived is the establishment of an association. And so it is with off-off Broadway. In January, 1972, several theatres got together to form OOBA, the Off-Off-Broadway Alliance. Like other special-interest associations, OOBA was formed as they put it, "to help its member theatres achieve their artistic goals." Funded by grants, and with an office of its own at 245 W.

52nd Street, NYC, the arrival of OOBA on the scene is one more sign that OOB has flourished.

Off-off-Broadway has been laughed at, ignored, humiliated, defeated, evicted, demolished, threatened, spit at, bankrupted, critically annihilated, demeaned, cheated, mugged, demoralized, blacked-out, locked-out, burglarized, walked out on, in short; raped. Yet every night in New York there's still an off-off-Broadway out there, a whole cloth of theatre that is very much in the thick—and thicket—of life and art. What is astonishing now is not that it goes on, but that it goes on while most New Yorkers and visitors to this city continue to be unaware of its amazing persistence, amazing creativity.

Despite this mass slap in the face, for ten years now OOB has been spreading like a mutant amoeba that is burgeoning far, far beyond its expected size. Plays, directors, producers, performers, lighting techs, costumers, stage hands, managers—they keep coming and going. An entire company may appear in October, with printed leaflets announcing its first production, along with a statement of its aims. And it may do just that for two, maybe even three productions, before silently folding its curtain and stealing away into the New York night.

Never to be heard from again? Not really. One of the great resources of OOB is that there is this continual flowing back and forth between companies and theatres. So if one company shuts down on West Fourth Street, chances are betting-good that many of the theatre's energies and know-how and materials will show up at the "stage door" of another unit on East 73rd Street. And sprinkled among several others. Some drop out of the current, others rejoin it. But the overall pattern continues; in this ability to regroup is its fountain of youth.

This pattern is particularly true of the performers, who by necessity and tradition, seek to perform as often as possible. Permanent repertory companies, while not unknown in OOB, are not common. New Re-

SPECIAL REPORT 9

pertory is one; the CSC is another; nevertheless there is always a very solid base of performing talent often experienced, usually spirited, that exists at any given time on OOB. But it is a living, changing source.

Judging from the number of theatres, and gauging from past activities, and taking into account that not all theatres appear in our rundown, a reasonable guess of the number of productions mounted each year off-off-Broadway is probably around 1,000. That's not performances, mind you. That's individual productions, each of which may offer anywhere from one to a thousand performances of its own.

Not only does OOB produce in great numbers. It produces more kinds of works: original, classical and modern plays, infrequently produced classical and modern plays—more plays than anywhere in the world. Think of that. More theatrical creation than anywhere. Most significant perhaps is that hundreds of new plays are aired out in off-off-Broadway houses each year. Frankly, some of them need all the airing they can get! At the same time, some of these writers, and some of their plays, may be worth remembering of this time and place in centuries to come. It is possible, in fact, that some of these writers are represented in this book.

But that's time's problem. Right now is seems more worthwhile to remember that those 1,000 productions represent many thousands of individual performances, and a few thousand rehearsals to go with them. And thousands of hours of auditions. And thousands more for costume-making. And thousands more for stage building, and prop borrowing. Playwriting, and adaptation. And thousands more for lighting. For the actors to prepare. And make-up making. Leaflet printing and ticket taking.

Millions of hours of mental and physical labor have been expended in an "industry" that has been in the red every year since its existence. And everyone involved knows it will continue to "operate" in the red. Everyone also knows it will continue to operate. For, of course, it is not an industry at all. It is a business of the spirit, and there can be little financial profit in stuff as intangible as that. But human profit *is* abundant here.

BEHIND-THE-SCENE

The Groups

1.

Robert Patrick, a playwright whose work is represented in these pages, has created an Off-Off Broadway hero named Haley Comet who frolics through the pages of *Proscenium,* a newsletter concerned with OOB events and issues. In a recent episode, Haley attended a meeting of "Playwrights for Playwrights," where the assembled members were handing out copies of play anthologies:

"Plethora held up Eels' new anthology, containing new plays by Plethora, Rachel, Houri, Mega, Moray and Uriah.

" 'That reminds me,' " said Uriah, 'I've got copies of my anthology too,' and he whipped out his, which contained works by Plethora, Rachel, Houri, Mega, Moray and Uriah.

" 'Look at mine, look at mine too,' " Rachel bawled. Hers held works by Plethora, Houri, Mega, Moray, Uriah and Eels."

Until publication last year of *The Scene/1,* the printing of plays from Off-Off Broadway was a classically incestuous situation. The same names appeared with such monotony that one had merely to hear one of the names to know which others would be represented. A cynic might even have supposed that the editor-playwrights (sometimes editor-critic-playwrights) were prudently selecting colleagues who might later put *their* work into an anthology. With few exceptions, the playwrights published in these collections emerged from the OOB of the sixties and saw their work produced at LaMama, Cafe Cino, Theatre Genesis and Judson.

But a new generation of playwrights has emerged from the OOB of the seventies; they are talented, they are provocative, they are frequently produced and their work enhances the printed page. For the most part, the editors of *The Scene* have focused on this "second generation" of OOB playwrights and theatres. (Ironically, the one Old Guard playwright is Patrick himself—but he is also the most frequently produced OOB playwright and he has yet to edit an anthology).

Nine playwrights were represented in *The Scene/1*. This current collection contains the works of fourteen playwrights—seven one-act plays, Act 1 of a full-length play, and five scenes from rather long works that could not be printed in full (one play is co-authored). Thus, more than twenty new playwrights are represented in the two collections—and that list will expand substantially with each future edition of *The Scene*. Each of these plays was actually *seen* by one of the editors or other staff members—we know they are "playing" plays as well as "reading" plays. In all cases, we have given full credit to the directors, actors, etc., involved in the productions, while also mentioning other productions wherever such information was available.

In selecting, we have tried to represent as best we could the enormously varied spectrum of Off-Off Broadway. Oscar Mandel's "Living Room With 6 Oppressions" and Patrick's "Simultaneous Transmissions" have a political orientation; Michael McGrinder's "We Hate To See You Go" is a black comedy; Sharon Thie's "Coffee Stand" etches the inherent explosiveness of everyday events; Sally Ordway's "Family, Family" has Women's Lib undertones. Arthur Sainer's "1 Piece Smash" and William Kushner's "Magic Time" have striking similarities. Both are one-character plays, both are uncompromisingly abrasive; the Sainer piece is virtual anti-theatre. You may not delight in or even accept the premises of these two plays, but you certainly can't ignore them. The sections from longer works range from the biblical milieu of Joseph Renard's "The Wrath Of God" to the modern urban misfortunes of Joseph Lazarus' "The New York Transit Authority."

In addition to the plays, another up-to-date report by Tom Tolnay and an expanded list of OOB theatres, *The Scene/2* contains two departments that were absent from the first collection: a photoessay of the OOB scene by Michael Campioni and a special section on theatre trends featuring comments by a representative sampling of artistic directors.

2.

One trend not mentioned in this special section but certainly worthy of comment is the emergence of playwright groups, notably the New York Theatre Strategy and the Playwrights Cooperative. Each of these groups has over twenty member-playwrights—and if Walter Kerr wants an incisive answer to his continual wail of "where are the new playwrights?" he should have been prowling Off-Off Broadway last spring. In June, the New York Theater Strategy held a four-week festival at the Manhattan Theatre Club in which each of its members was represented. The Playwrights Cooperative, not to be outdone, held a three-month festival (April through June) at over a dozen OOB theatres.

There are several positive aspects to these groups and these festivals. They have proven that playwrights are more than capable of handling their own productions. They have publicized the merits of Off-Off Broadway to a previously uninitiated audience. Perhaps most importantly, by involving so many actors, directors, artistic directors and technical people in a concerted effort, they have at least temporarily reversed some of the ingrown factionalism that has typically hampered New York theatre. The Playwrights Cooperative festival in particular seemed to foster an ecumenical spirit that is remarkable in what is certainly not the least ruthless of theatre environments.

Nevertheless, transient feelings of good fellowship cannot paper over some very substantial differences between the two groups or the very real dangers of playwright-conglomerates that function as lobbies. And there can be little question that the New York Theatre Strategy *is* a lobby. Without exception, it is composed of the Old Guard playwrights who put each other's works in each other's anthologies. Foster, Wilson, Shepherd, Fornes, Ravel, Mednick, Owens—one has only to list some of the member-playwrights, and the "hip" observer can round out the membership roll almost by rote.

These are playwrights who have been produced at all of the prestigious Off-Off houses; they are published not only in anthologies but in individual collections of their works; many have had successful Off-Broadway and even Broadway productions; their plays are presented in Europe and in every corner of the globe; their work and style is holy writ in many of our more important universities, and they have monopolized the media to such an extent that the "outside world" knows and hears little of other OOB playwrights.

Why, then, do these playwrights need a *group?* One answer is that they have been screwed over and over by producers and theatre owners and now wish to control their own destinies. But there is another, insidious reason that is almost never mentioned: the Strategy playwrights consider themselves the Establishment of OOB, indeed of New York theatre and even world theatre. With all their talk about "avant-garde," they have become the status quo—and they don't intend to relinquish any of the power, prestige and publicity they have captured over the past dozen or so years.

A good example of this lobbying technique was a recent article by Tom Eyen in the *Sunday Times* theatre section. Written in characteristic Eyencamp, the article depicts a scene in which the author is waiting for all of the gifted OOB playwrights to arrive for dinner. Dutifully, all of the Strategy playrights are mentioned and all eventually appear. The article ends with a murky denouement in which

THE GROUPS

the playrights are sitting in a darkened room watching a movie and thinking back wistfully to the Good Old Days of OOB.

The unremitting intent of this article is to project the concept that the Strategy playwrights *are* Off-Off Broadway; no other OOB playwrights are permitted to exist, and if they do exist they must be inconsequential. If you weren't *there* when Paul Foster said "Hi" to Sam Shepherd or when Joe Cino polished his first coffee machine, you simply don't rate as an OOB playwright. If you don't belong to the Strategy, you don't belong—because we say so. The *Sunday Times* apparently shares this attitude; it has yet to grant a similar platform to a member of the Playwrights Cooperative or any other playwright group.

The Strategy has a powerful ally in Michael Smith of the *Village Voice,* who functions as its not-so-unofficial spokesman and den mother. Smith has devoted several columns to the Strategy and its individual playwrights. When he attended the Strategy Festivals opening night, Smith tells us, it was like Old Home Week; all of the *important* people of OOB were there and naturally the review was glowing.

While Smith is favorably disposed to most of the Strategy playwrights, he seems to have particular li'l darlings who can do no wrong. If a new play by Ronald Tavel, Murray Mednick or Charles Ludlam is opening, Smith is usually there and the review is usually rave. If the play is opening at Theatre Genesis, where Smith also directs, the review is likely to be rapturous. On the rare occasions when he cannot attend, Smith is there hovering in the background, ready to swoop like a mother-hawk on the offending critic who might dare criticize his fledglings.

A particularly ludicrous example of Smith's overprotectiveness occurred when fellow *Voice* critic Michael Feingold reviewed Charles Ludlam's production of *Camille*. Feingold wrote that he was skeptical and unconvinced about Ludlam's playing Camille in drag. The next week, Smith countered that Feingold was misinformed; Ludlam was not in drag at all but was simply portraying Camille. Feingold then commented that Smith should have his eyes examined if he thought that Charles Ludlam was really a woman, whereupon Smith, summoning all of his weight and authority, declared that Ludlam could not only play Camille but had an "historic right" to play Camille. While this momentous debate was going on, many worthy productions went unreviewed and unnoted by the *Village Voice*.

None of this is meant to denigrate Smith's singular contribution to the early development of Off-Off Broadway. Were it not for Smith and other *Voice* critics such as Robert Pasoli, OOB would never have gotten off the ground in the sixties and might well have vanished altogether. Further, when he foregos the press-agentry, Smith can be an extremely intelligent and perceptive critic—considerably more magnanimous than his *Voice* colleagues who often seem to be competing for a Derisive Review of the Year award.

When we turn to the Playwright's Cooperative, we encounter an entirely different set of equations. For the most part, these are "second generation" playwrights—and it's no accident that several of them appear in this collection and in *The Scene/1*. While these playwrights have had quite as many productions in recent years as the Strategy playwrights and have demonstrated their talent, they are rarely given the media attention commensurate with this talent. They are just now starting to get published, and many appear on the verge of gaining some notice outside of their own circle.

Several Cooperative playwrights already have received such notice—notably Obie Award winner Richard Foreman, OOB veteran Donald Kvares, and internationally-produced Mario Fratti—and this can only encourage the other Cooperative playwrights about their own futures. Put in the plainest terms, the Cooperative playwrights want what the Strategy playwrights already have and are loathe to share.

THE GROUPS

It was perhaps perfectly natural that they banded together to pursue this goal.

The key figure in the Playwrights Cooperative unquestionably is Arthur Sainer. Both a playwright and a *Village Voice* critic, Sainer has been spoken of as the founder of the group, although Kvares was apparently responsible for much of the original impetus. Unlike Michael Smith, Sainer makes no bones about being an *official,* active, functioning member of his group. It's much to his credit that he did not review any of the productions in the Playwrights Cooperative festival; he *was* instrumental in getting other *Voice* critics down to these shows, but the reviews were by no means uniformly favorable. Moreover, Sainer's appearance at non-festival productions of his members' plays is no guarantee of a good review—he is as likely to drub the production as to praise it.

But whatever Sainer's efforts at objectivity, there may be something unkosher about a playwrights group that is this "plugged in" to the *Village Voice*. Sainer was able to obtain considerable *Voice* publicity for the Playwrights Cooperative festival and the fact is that, good reviews or bad, *Voice* critics did attend most of the productions. This has to be irritating to the many capable OOB playwrights outside the pale of either group, several of whom have six or seven productions and never see a *Voice* critic. Consider that there may be as many as seventy-five OOB productions going on simultaneously and that the *Voice* is the only major newspaper that covers Off-Off on a regular basis, and you begin to see why the fifty or so Cooperative and Strategy playwrights want an inside track on getting a *Voice* review.

It would be interesting to see what would happen if a third playwrights group—Patrick's "Playwrights for Playwrights," for example—decided to have a festival. Would these playwrights be interviewed by Michael Smith? Would free publicity be available in various *Voice* columns? Would *Voice* critics dutifully attend and review the plays?

At this juncture, it would seem that the Playwrights Cooperative has a great capacity for either good or nongood. If it merely seeks to replace one OOB Establishment with another, it will be a total disappointment. If it seeks to foster a new openness on Off-Off Broadway and a continuation of the ecumenical spirit it introduced last spring, it can be the spearhead of what Sainer himself has called "the true community of theatre."

Stanley Nelson, *Editor*
Harry Smith, *Publisher*

We Hate to See You Go

MICHAEL MCGRINDER

WE HATE TO SEE YOU GO was seen at the Old Reliable Theatre Tavern, 231 East 3rd Street, New York City, in August, 1970. The production was directed by Michael McGrinder, Set Design was by Judy Pendleton, Lighting Design by Joanna Schielke and the Technical Supervisor was Mary Sterling. The play featured the following actors:

TIM REILLY	Stephen Harrison
NOLAN	Harry Orzello
EILEEN REILLY	M. A. Whiteside
JOSIE REILLY	Francine Middleton
NEIL REILLY	Joseph Downing

© 1968 by Michael McGrinder

CAUTION: You are hereby warned that WE HATE TO SEE YOU GO is subject to a royalty. It is fully protected under the copyright laws of the United States of America and all countries of the Copyright Union. All rights, including professional, amateur, motion picture, recitation, lecturing, public reading, radio broadcasting, television and the rights of translation into foreign languages are strictly reserved. In its present form, the play is dedicated only to the reading public.
This play may be presented only upon payment of a royalty whether admission is charged or not. Permission for all readings, amateur or professional, must be applied for in writing.
All inquiries concerning rights should be addressed to the author's representative: Barbara Rhodes, Kahn, Lifflander & Rhodes, Inc., 853 Seventh Avenue, New York, N.Y. 10019.

Approximate playing time: 30 minutes

Nolan's Funeral Parlor. An empty coffin. Chairs—of the folding variety—as needed. Flowers—at least one wreath with a ribbon of white, preferably near head of coffin. TIM REILLY *is knotting his black tie sans mirror. He wears the trousers of a dark blue suit and a white shirt.* NOLAN, *the undertaker, enters, brushing the jacket of* REILLY'S *suit.*

NOLAN: Here, let me. *He lays jacket on coffin and starts to help with tie.*

REILLY: *pulling away.* I'm not helpless. *He finishes with tie which is somewhat askew.* NOLAN *slowly shakes his head.* Oh, Jesus. REILLY *allows the adjustment to be made.*

NOLAN: Mind your language, now. You'll never get to heaven taking the Lord's name in vain.

REILLY: I can no longer commit sin. Mortal or venial.

NOLAN: Doesn't the good man fall seven times a day?

REILLY: I've fallen for the last time. It's out of my hands now.

NOLAN: Perhaps. It's not for me to judge. *He removes jacket from coffin.* Here, get into your shroud.

REILLY: *donning jacket.* Can I have some now? NOLAN *steps back to survey* REILLY.

NOLAN: No more. *Pause.* I wish people would wear black shrouds. They're more in keeping with the dignity of it all.

REILLY: Doesn't make much difference to me what color it is. Just a drop?

NOLAN: You've had enough. Any more and you'll be singing during prayers. *Pause.* They hate black shrouds. It always has to be dark blue or grey. They don't want to face the truth.

REILLY: They're supposed to be happy you're in Paradise.

NOLAN: Paradise? You don't really think you're . . .

REILLY: And why not? *Pause.* If I can't have any more fluid I'll get up and ask for some. They'd expect that, wouldn't they, never believing you're gone.

NOLAN: *sighs.* Just a drop, then. *He gets a whiskey bottle and two glasses from under the coffin.*

REILLY: Anyone would think it was you.

NOLAN: I have respect for the dead. I never like to see a man drink alone.

REILLY: Here's luck, then.

NOLAN: Cheers. *They drink and* NOLAN *starts to take* REILLY's *glass.*

REILLY: Just one more. A drop, that's all.

NOLAN: You will behave?

REILLY: Just a drop. NOLAN *fills both glasses and they drink.*

NOLAN: There's one thing I have to hand you, Tim. You do face facts. It's an admirable trait. So few are willing.

REILLY: Not a bloody sight much I can do.

NOLAN: *putting bottle and glasses away.* No, but you should see some we get. They want no part of it.

REILLY: Know where they're going, no doubt.

NOLAN: They grow so you can't get them in the box and you have to shave them and clip their nails. Then they sit up and scare the daylights out of people. They're not like the Chinese at all. Why, the Chinese often drop dead in the rice fields and go right on working until somebody takes them away. Don't want to cause anybody any trouble, the Chinese.

REILLY: Tough little bastards. I recall an uncle of mine who was dead for three weeks before we found out about it. We fixed his wagon for him, though. Didn't give him a bite to eat. Breakfast, lunch and supper—an empty plate was all he got for a week after we found out. He finally realized he wouldn't get anything to eat unless he owned up and died a Christian death.

NOLAN: How did you find out?

REILLY: *holding his nose.* After three weeks?

NOLAN: *nods and looks at watch.* Speaking of time, Tim.

REILLY: What's your hurry? Trying to get rid of me?

NOLAN: They'll be here soon.

REILLY: Just one more corpse to sling in the dirt, then get on to the next.

NOLAN: I've treated you decent. Now be a Christian and get in the box.

REILLY: Jesus, you must make a fortune. That's what I should have been . . .

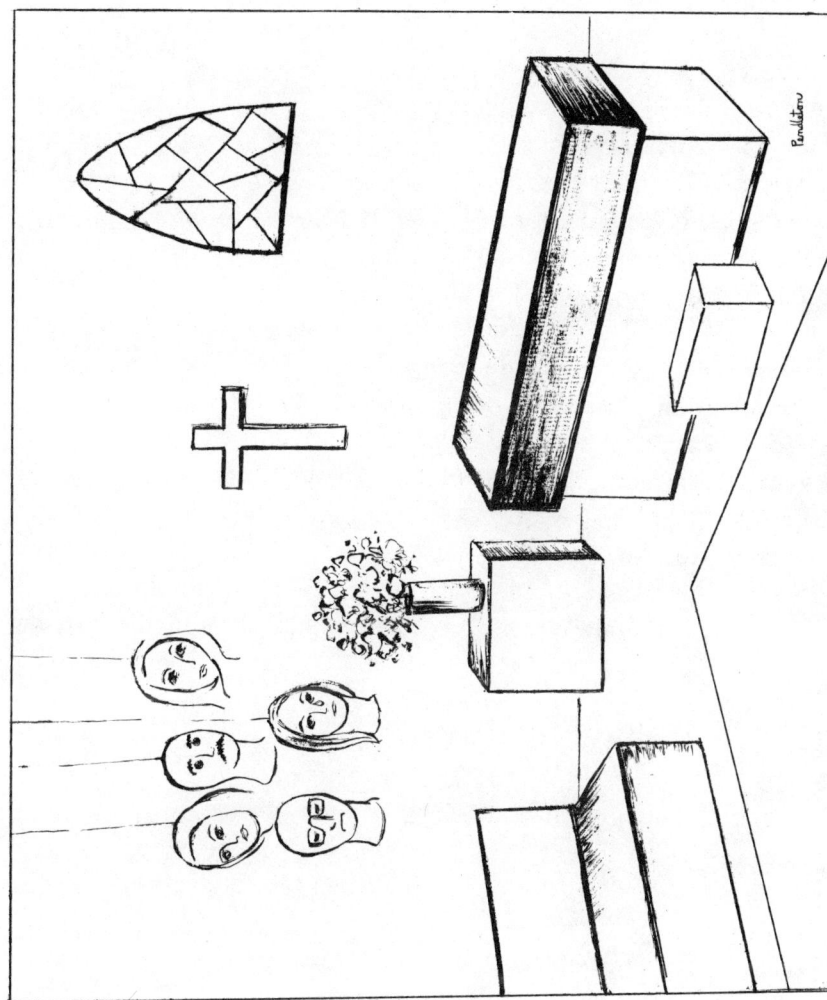

Set design by Judy Pendleton for 'We Hate To See You Go,' performed at Old Reliable.

NOLAN: Get in the box!

REILLY: . . . an undertaker. A fortune. And always a nip to be found.

NOLAN: You're afraid.

REILLY: Who's afraid?

NOLAN: You are. You're afraid to get in the box.

REILLY: And why should I be afraid of a box?

NOLAN: Because I'm going to put it in the ground with you in it and throw dirt on you and the worms are going to eat you up.

REILLY: I'm not afraid of that. Can I have a small one?

NOLAN: No! Now get in the box!

REILLY: You're always quick enough to put others in the box, but nobody ever sees you in it.

NOLAN: I'm alive.

REILLY: That's no excuse for being a coward.

NOLAN: I am not afraid of getting in the box.

REILLY: You're afraid of being buried in it and letting the worms get you.

NOLAN: Nobody's going to bury me. I'm alive. *Pause.*

REILLY: It's happened.

NOLAN: You're impossible. Now get in the box, you Goddamned stiff!

REILLY: Have some respect for the dead. Prove you're not afraid. Get in the box yourself.

NOLAN: I'll do nothing of the kind.

REILLY: You're afraid. I knew it. Scaredy-cat! Scaredy-cat!

NOLAN: Stop it! Stop!

REILLY: *childishly.* The undertaker's afraid of the box! The undertaker's afraid of the box! The undertaker's afraid of the box!

NOLAN: *firmly.* I am not afraid of the box.

REILLY: Prove it. *Long pause.*

NOLAN: All right. *He gets bottle and a glass and pours a drink which he downs quickly.*

REILLY: Can I . . .

NOLAN: No. *NOLAN puts the bottle and glass away and stands at the side of the coffin. The lights dim while the area surrounding the coffin is bathed in a soft blue light. Now, then . . . NOLAN wipes his hands on a handkerchief, then grips the edge of the coffin. Pause. Slowly he climbs into the coffin where he assumes a kneeling position.* Satisfied?

REILLY: Lie down. *NOLAN lies on his stomach.* On your back. *NOLAN turns over.* Now fold your hands. *NOLAN folds his hands.*

NOLAN: Satisfied? *REILLY grips the coffin lid and starts to lower it. NOLAN sits up quickly.* What are you trying to do? *REILLY forces him down again and NOLAN tries to fight him off.*

The lights change instantly back to normal. REILLY's *family is at the door: his wife—*EILEEN, *his daughter—*JOSIE, *his brother—*NEIL. *They survey the scene a moment.*

EILEEN: Timothy!

JOSIE: Daddy!

NEIL: Jesus, Mary and Joseph! REILLY *stops fighting and turns sheepishly to his family.*

NOLAN: He won't get in the box, Mrs. Reilly.

JOSIE: How can he?

NOLAN *scrambles out of the coffin.* EILEEN *goes to* REILLY, *takes his ear in her hand and leads him toward the coffin.*

EILEEN: I don't know what you think you're up to, Timothy Reilly, but you can march straight into that box before I box you one on the ears.

REILLY: Leggo, Goddamnit.

EILEEN: The box.

REILLY: Have some respect for the dead.

EILEEN: *releasing him.* All right, since you put it that way, but get in there and stop shaming me.

NEIL: Come on, Tim. I'll give you a hand.

REILLY: *pushing him away.* I can manage. *He approaches coffin, poises his hands over its edge. Pause.*

JOSIE: Go on, Daddy. You can do it!

REILLY: STOP RUSHING ME!

NOLAN *whispers to* NEIL *who nods assent. They motion for the ladies to get out of the way, then they approach* REILLY *from behind, pick him up and put him in the coffin while he struggles against them. They finally get him settled and move away. Lights dim. Blue light on coffin.* REILLY *sits up.*

REILLY: I'll see the lot of you in hell. *Nobody takes any notice of him and he lies down.*

NOLAN: *to the family.* Shall we?

They all kneel and bow their heads. With the exception of JOSIE, *who sneaks over to the coffin, they sing:*

NOLAN, EILEEN, NEIL: *slowly.* We hate to see you go.
                      We hate to see you go.
                lively. We hope to hell you never come back.
                slowly. We hate to see you go.

JOSIE, *during the singing, kisses her father and climbs in the coffin with him.* EILEEN *looks up.*

EILEEN: Josie! *Lights return to normal.* Get out of there at once!

JOSIE: I want to go with him.

NEIL: You daft bitch. That's your mother's job.

NOLAN: Get out! ! ! Get out!

NEIL *and* NOLAN *drag* JOSIE, *screaming, out of the coffin.*

JOSIE: I want to go with him. Let me go with him!

EILEEN: You just sit there and behave yourself. JOSIE *sits heavily on the floor in front of the coffin.*

JOSIE: You never let me do what I want. Daddy's the only one who ever loved me. If he were still alive I'd tell him about you and Uncle Neil.

EILEEN: Have some respect for the dead.

JOSIE: I'm sorry, Uncle Neil. NEIL *puts his arms around* EILEEN.

NEIL: You're sending him out in grand style, Eileen. He'd be proud of you.

EILEEN: I wanted him to have the best.

NEIL: The coffin must cost a fortune itself.

NOLAN: Two thousand dollars, Mr. Reilly.

Pause.

EILEEN: I thought you told me one thousand.

NOLAN: Two thousand.

EILEEN: One thousand.

NOLAN: Two thousand.

EILEEN: One thousand.

NEIL: It's a poor time to argue about money. Why don't you just compromise? Say, fifteen hundred.

NOLAN: Fifteen hundred ... If it's all right with Mrs. Reilly ...

EILEEN: It's best that way, isn't it? Fifteen hundred, then.

JOSIE: You're both five hundred dollars better off.

EILEEN: She always was such a bright child.

JOSIE: How much are the gloves?

NOLAN: Forty-five dollars a pair.

EILEEN: What gloves?

NOLAN: For the pallbearers, Mrs. Reilly. Four pairs.

EILEEN: Four times forty-five dollars. Why, that's ... that's ...

NEIL: Outrageous.

JOSIE: One hundred and eighty dollars.

EILEEN: ONE HUNDRED AND EIGHTY DOLLARS! ! ! ? ?

JOSIE: The gloves for Aunt Nora's funeral cost sixty dollars a pair.

NEIL: Sixty dollars? Who buried her? JOSIE *nods toward* NOLAN.

EILEEN: *to* NOLAN. Sixty dollars! And you charge us forty-five. Mr. Nolan, do we look like paupers?

NOLAN: Why, of course not, Mrs. Reilly. I didn't realize ...

EILEEN: I told you I wanted my husband to go out in style, Mr. Nolan, and I meant *style*.

NOLAN: Well, will sixty-five be all right? *Pause.* Seventy? *Pause.*

Eighty-five? *Pause.* A hundred. I won't go any higher.

EILEEN: Eighty-five will do nicely, thank you.

JOSIE: Three hundred and forty dollars, just for four pairs of gloves . . . That's not including state and city sales tax.

NEIL: You'd never be able to pay for this, Eileen, if Tim hadn't died and left you the insurance.

Lights dim. Blue glow on coffin. REILLY *sits up.*

REILLY: Is nobody going to pay their respects to the dead? *He lies down.*

NOLAN: You first, Mrs. Reilly.

EILEEN: I can't. I can't bear to look at him.

NOLAN: *leading her forcibly to the coffin.* Now, he isn't that bad.

NOLAN *withdraws.* NEIL *puts a comforting arm around him and leads him to the side.*

NOLAN: She forgets my position in this. Thinks only of herself.

NEIL: Sssh! I want to see if the widow breaks down.

EILEEN: *at coffin.* He was such a good man. I look at him and I can't help wondering what he's thinking about Neil and me. *She kneels.* Forgive me, Tim. I'm a lonely widow who needs to be around a man.

REILLY: *without moving.* What about when I was alive?

EILEEN: You look so fine, Tim. The picture of health. You'll be happy to know that Neil and me don't have to sneak behind your back anymore. We can get married now you're gone. You do give us your blessing, don't you, Tim? Say you do. *She rises and takes his face in her hands. She kisses him and begins to weep.* Give me a sign, Tim. Say something. A sign. Just give me a sign.

REILLY *makes a suggestive gesture.* EILEEN *slaps at the raised hand.*

EILEEN: You son of a bitch! NOLAN *and* NEIL *both rush to her, pulling her away from the coffin.* He never was any good. He didn't die. He just rotted away.

NEIL: Eileen, watch your mouth.

EILEEN: Oh. I'm sorry, Mr. Nolan. I must have been hysterical. What must you think of me?

NOLAN: Nothing to think, Mrs. Reilly. They're all like that.

EILEEN: The corpses?

NOLAN: The widows.

JOSIE *approaches the coffin, kneels, makes the sign of the cross.*

JOSIE: Bless me, father, for I have sinned. It has been one month since my last confession.

EILEEN: Josie!

NOLAN: The poor child's out of her senses with grief. Try again, dear.

EILEEN: She told me she went to confession last Saturday.

JOSIE: I don't know what they want, Daddy . . . I . . . I'm supposed to do something, I know, but I can't remember what it is . . . I feel cold . . . I'd like to get in with you and get warm . . . Mommy won't let me, though . . . She says I'm too big . . . too big to sleep with men anymore. I'd like to just the same. *Rising.* Oh, Daddy. You'll keep me warm, won't you, Daddy?

JOSIE *starts to get in the coffin.* EILEEN *screams and rushes at her, dragging her away. Lights return to normal.*

JOSIE: I want my Daddy!

EILEEN: He is not your Daddy.

JOSIE: How would you know?

EILEEN: I just know, that's all. Women have ways of knowing such things. You'll understand eventually.

JOSIE: I don't believe you. I don't believe there's any way of telling.

NEIL: Your mother knows best, Josie.

NOLAN: Have some respect for your mother.

JOSIE: Daddy's my daddy. You didn't know. Not any of you. We kept it secret. Just the two of us. *Toward coffin.* Didn't we, Daddy?

Pause, as they all turn toward coffin, expectantly.

NEIL: So, you have no proof.

JOSIE: I have. My name is Reilly, isn't it?

EILEEN: Who told you that?

JOSIE: At school. The nuns told me. I told them I didn't have a daddy and they slapped my face and asked me if anybody slept with my mother and when I told them I did, they asked me if anybody else did.

EILEEN: For God's sake, you didn't tell them!

JOSIE: They were nuns. I couldn't lie to them. The devil would come and take me away if I did. I told them that sometimes, when I slept with you, I'd wake up in the morning and find Daddy in the bed with me.

EILEEN: That sneaking son of a . . . still, we were all pretty happy for a while.

JOSIE: The nuns whispered to each other then. They said that if it was Daddy who was in my bed then it would be Daddy who was my daddy. Then, when they showed me how to write my name they found out I was left-handed so they made me write with my right hand.

EILEEN: I don't believe it.

JOSIE: They did. That's why I'm so bright today.

NEIL: The nuns must have known what they were doing.

NOLAN: You can't question the clergy.

EILEEN: Nuns aren't clergy.

NEIL: They're the priests' wives, aren't they? *NEIL crosses to coffin as he speaks. He stares at REILLY. Lights dim. Blue glow on coffin area.*

NEIL: Tim, lad . . . *He takes REILY's hand in his own.* Jesus, Tim, the times we had. Gone. All gone. The time we . . . *Laughs.* . . . Oh, God, do you recall the night we . . *Laughs louder.* . . . And the time Mrs. . . . *Laughs louder with less control.* REILLY *sits up.*

REILLY: And what about the time you . . . *They laugh together.*

NEIL: And . . .

They laugh louder, more hysterically.

REILLY: Jesus, and . . . *They are now completely hysterical and out of control.* NOLAN *approaches and tries to separate them.*

NOLAN: Please, Mr. Reilly.

NEIL AND REILLY: *together.* Which one?

NEIL *and* REILLY *punch each other good-naturedly on the shoulder.*

EILEEN: Timothy! You're making a fool of me.

JOSIE: Hit him one for me, Daddy!

REILLY *and* NEIL *bang each other on the shoulder several times, their laughter fading as they grow serious, hitting harder, getting more and more intense.*

REILLY: Hit a man while he's down.

NEIL: Still trying to pick on me. Ever since we were kids.

REILLY: I blame you for my death.

NEIL: I hope you rot in hell. REILLY'*s last blow knocks* NEIL *down.*

REILLY *lies down in the coffin and the lights come on as normal.* NOLAN *assumes the pose of a prize-fight referee over* NEIL.

NOLAN: One . . . two . . . three . . . four . . .

EILEEN: The poor man. He's collapsed with greed. *quickly.* Grief.

NOLAN: Five . . . six . . . seven . . . NEIL *stirs and sits up. He gets on his knees.* Eight . . . nine . . . NEIL *rises quickly, doing a little boxing-dance.*

NEIL: Not this time, Mr. Nolan.

NOLAN *shrugs and goes to coffin. He wipes* REILLY'*s brow with a handerchief, straightens* REILLY'*s tie, smooths back his hair.*

JOSIE: *yawns.* I'm bored. Why don't we go home and come back in time for the end.

EILEEN: Because we're the immediate family.

NOLAN: If you're restless, Mrs. Reilly, might I suggest you go out for a drink? It might relax you. NEIL *turns an imploring look toward* EILEEN.

EILEEN: *at, rather than to,* NEIL. None of us drink.

NEIL: I do.

EILEEN: Not if you want to play cards tonight, big boy.

JOSIE: I'll play cards with you, Uncle Neil.

EILEEN: You don't know how to play cards, dear.

JOSIE: I do so. I play cards all the time.

EILEEN: And just where did you learn to play?

JOSIE: I watched you and Uncle Neil. *Giggles.* I never let you know I was watching.

NEIL: That settles it, then.

EILEEN: Three-handed gin.

JOSIE: Oh, Mommy! Thank you!

NOLAN: *shyly.* I play cards too, Mrs. Reilly.

JOSIE: Which game do you play, Mr. Nolan?

NOLAN: *sheepishly.* Solitaire.

EILEEN *clamps her hands over* JOSIE's *ears and stares at* NOLAN *who backs away, astonished by her reaction. He bumps into the coffin.* REILLY *sits up and glares at him. Lights dim. Blue glow on coffin.*

REILLY: You gettin' wise with my kid? NOLAN *tries to force* REILLY *to lie down and* REILLY *pushes him away.*

NOLAN: Lie down, Mr. Reilly. Please.

REILLY: *folding his arms.* Make me.

NOLAN: Please, Mr. Reilly. Don't force me to get violent.

The family gathers around, watching. NOLAN *pushes back his sleeves and approaches the coffin, stopping just out of* REILLY's *reach.*

NOLAN: You've asked for it now. I'm going to put you in the ground and cover you up and leave you to the worms.

REILLY: It's not time.

NOLAN: The worms!

REILLY: It's not time! *To the others.* Don't let him do it. It's not time yet!

NEIL: Be brave, Tim!

JOSIE: *snivelling.* Daddy. Oh, Daddy.

NOLAN: I can see you going down now into the hole.

REILLY: *screaming.* No! Give me time!

NOLAN: The chink-chink of dirt hitting the coffin lid.

REILLY: Help me! Somebody help me!

NOLAN: The rain falling at night in the graveyard. The owls screeching. Whoo! Whoo! Whoo!

EILEEN: I can't bear it!

NOLAN: The worms eating the box, getting into the lining, to your epidermis, devouring you bit by bit. You rot, Reilly. You rot in your expensive box and you stink to high heaven. Little by little you're carried away in the belly of the worms and turned into fertilizer. You rot!

REILLY: Save me! Help me! Please!

EILEEN: STOP!

Lights return quickly to normal.

NOLAN: It's too late to stop.

NEIL: She's footing the bill.

NOLAN: You'll have to give back the insurance.

EILEEN: You've got it all. EILEEN *and* JOSIE *have gone to the coffin. They help* REILLY *to climb out. He leans, trembling and weak, on their shoulders.*

REILLY: Save me from the worms.

JOSIE: It's all right, Daddy. It's us.

NEIL: You're going home, boy. Home!

REILLY: Home . . . Are there worms at home?

JOSIE: Only the woodworm . . . in the bed.

NOLAN: Put him back! You can't stop it!

EILEEN: *to* REILLY. Don't tremble, darling. We're taking you home. You can sleep in your own bed with your own wife.

JOSIE: Can I get in too, Mommy?

EILEEN: Of course you can, dear.

JOSIE: Oh, thank you. We'll keep you warm, Daddy.

NOLAN: *shouting.* What about when he rots?

NEIL: He was rotten a long time ago.

EILEEN *and* JOSIE *go off with* REILLY. NEIL *stares at* NOLAN. NOLAN *pushes down his sleeves, smiles at* NEIL *who turns to leave and bumps into coffin. Blue glow comes on coffin as* NEIL *screams and runs off. Lights, except for light on coffin, begin to dim.* NOLAN *stares after* NEIL.

NOLAN: Good-bye . . . Mr. Reilly.

NOLAN *looks out at audience, his head turning slowly from left to right. Almost in darkness now, he stares straight into audience, smiles widely, and advances a step toward them.*

BLACKOUT

Magic Time

WILLIAM KUSHNER

> MAGIC TIME was seen at the Cubiculo, 414 West 51st Street, New York City, in May, 1973. The production was directed by Frederick Bailey and acted by William Kushner.
>
> Other productions: Dove Company, April, 1972, directed by Penny Peck; University of the Streets, March 1970, directed by **Ted Mornel**.
>
> *Approximate playing time: 23 minutes*

MISS VICTORIA: *off.* And now—it's Miss Victoria's MAGIC TIME! *Pause.* And here she is, kids—here I am—in person and myself—MISS VICTORIA!!

She enters . . . the magic lady, in pink gown . . . carrying magic wand. Too bad, though, she seems a bit soused.

Applause! Applause!
    Bows.
Bow! Bow! Bow-wow! Bow-wow!
    Falls down. Gets up with some difficulty.

Well—and where are all my children, my lovely, lovely children . . . come to hear their lovely Miss Victoria read to them another lovely, lovely story straight from Magic-Land?

Peers out.

Oh! There you all are! Well, hi, kids!

Pause for response.

Dear, dear children . . . I just know you're going to pay all your mind to today's story . . . because it's a true story . . . really it is . . . cross my heart—*She tries, but just sort of succeeds in slapping her breast about*—and it is so sweet, too!

Looks at breast.

Oh, the story, I mean, you naughty things! Yes! I wrote it myself, and it is lovely, because it really, really happened . . . to me!

Giggles, then, with a flutter of her wand.

Well, here we go, kids! It's Magic Time! Now shut u-up!

Picks up book, then peeks over top.

I see you!

Starts reading.

Once upon a time there was a man who always walked around with his head shaking, saying no, no, NO! Well! One day, guess what he bumped into! Give up? Well, one day he bumped his head shaking saying no into another man who always walked around with his head shaking, saying yes, yes, YES!

Looks up.

Did you get that, kids? Wasn't that funny? I think that's rather amusing. Don't you? *Pause.* Anyway—

Back to story.

"Hey, are you crazy or something?" the man who walks around with his head saying yes says. "Hey, are you crazy or something?" the man who walks around with his head saying no says. Well! They just stood there, I mean, stood there just glaring fit to kill at each other, their heads wagging yes, saying no. Well, naturally, a great big crowd of people began to gather . . . and, naturally, everyone began taking sides, not to mention a few bets, I bet, as to who's fault it was . . .

MAGIC TIME

Waves her wand.

Suddenly, the darlingest girl came along. And guess what? She had this thing, you know? This thing about saying "maybe"—

Sexy.

"Maybe!"

Licking her lips.

She had been out walking her doggie . . . oh, the sweetest, cutest doggie in the whole, wide world, I tell you!

Giggles.

Bow-wow! Bow-wow!

Giggles.

"I saw it all happen!" the darling girl said, as her doggie barked and barked and ran around the park peeing and peeing on all the trees freely . . .

Giggles.

"No, you are not wanted here," says the man with his head saying no. "Yes, everybody is wanted here," says the man with his head saying yes, "because this is a very important meeting. We may even collect contributions after it. Nobody leaves. Right?"

Giggles.

Well, the upshot was, they decided to take the issue up to the U.N. . . . that's short for United Nations, kids . . .

Pause, she reflects.

Isn't there a lovely sound to that? —United Nations—!

Pause.

Well, the UN decided to put the issue to a vote, which they did, and of course everybody disagreed. The representative from Russia wrote on his vote: "Uncle Sam is a cock-sucker!" To which, kids, our United States representative replied: "Yeah? Well, that may be true, but there are good cock-suckers and there are bad cock-suckers and you Ruskies are very very bad cock-suckers!"

To children. Pause.

Well, then what happened, children, was that right then and there the UN declared that there was to be a cock-sucking contest! And

so there was nothing else for the world to do just lay back to await the outcome!
Takes out bottle from purse.
Excuse me, just one tiny little minitie!
Wand gets in way.
Oh, this fucking wand! It's always getting in the way!
Takes drink.
Mmm! Wow, I needed that! *Pause.* Gosh, kids, your Magic Lady sure gets hot sometimes . . . under these hot lights, I mean. Oh, and this stupid-looking nightmare they make me wear doesn't help any!
Indicating gown.
Look at this! Will you look at this? I am so sick of this pink thing! I hate this pink thing! I hate PINK!
Pause.
Oh, yes, that feels so much better! I have been wanting to do that for years!
Looks down at her body, then up.
Yes, kids, this is me! Magical . . . me! Listen, you don't mind, do you, kids, just for tonight? I mean, I guess I'm sort of letting down my hair . . .
She does just that, removing her ping magic wig.
I mean, it feels so good . . . just to be free like this! Really, it does! Why don't you try it, too, kids, huh? Join me! I mean, be free, wherever you are . . . free!
Looks at book.
Now where the heck was I when we left off? Oh, yes —
Giggles.
"Aren't you both behaving kind of silly, maybe?" the darling girl who had a thing about saying maybe said. "After all," she said, "why get into an argument over nothing at all instead of something at all—like maybe me?" she said. "No, never," said the man with his no head. "Yes, never," said the other man with our darling girl . . . "cause if you both listen only to me, well, maybe I'll tell you both what happened." Well, I guess she thought she had just said some-

thing pretty funny, because suddenly our darling girl began to giggle! And the darling girl's doggie peed on the no man's knees and on the yes man's knees, and I guess the doggie thought that was pretty funny, because suddenly the doggie began to giggle. And for no reason whatsoever as far as I can see—the no man giggled and then the yes man giggled . . . and the world . . . yes, when they all three looked around, what do you think they saw? The world—the whole world—giggling! I tell you! Why, even the sun . . . even the sun came out and giggled a little. Well, after a period of time, of course, the giggles stopped giggling, but nevertheless, everyone still kinda sorta felt them there . . . in the air . . . waiting . . . to begin again . . .

Coughs, takes drink

Gosh, that part almost makes me want to cry! I mean, I just feel like —

Catches herself.

Oh, stop it, Magic Lady! You're behaving silly! And here! You can't do that here—in front of all your children . . . your lovely, lovely children . . . !

Drinks.

I am not a mother in real life! Well, I guess you didn't know that before . . . ! Well, now you do . . . ! And that's the whole idea really, of all of the stories I have bring to you —

Catches herself.

— I have brought to you. So you can know something about the magical world around you. Well, I mean, every story has a moral. Just like every person on this earth has a purpose, and every life, every life has a meaning—!

Pause.

I am nobody's mother in real life.

Pause.

Goodness!

Back to story.

"What happened was," the maybe girl said, "you were walking along with your silly head saying no and you were walking along with your silly head saying yes and in the middle of a no and in the middle of a yes you both bumped your beanies together, that's all! And, if you ask me, I think maybe it was bound to happen sooner or later . . .

Looks up.

Isn't she a clever, darling girl? Well, she thinks she is! And maybe she is!

Back to story.

"Are you sure you saw," no said. "Swear you're sure you saw," yes said. "Maybe I did maybe I didn't," our miss maybe girl said, "and what are you boys going to do about it, huh?"

Giggles.

Well, the cock-sucking contest was still going on over at the United Nations, so while they awaited the decision, the boys both took her out to lunch and over the soup, guess what, yes stopped his head just for a second to sip and over the nuts, guess what, no stopped his head a bit to buts and they all three had to agree they'd had a rather pleasant spree.

Waves bottle.

Whoopee! And then they took miss clever darling maybe girl home. "Maybe," she said, "you boys wanna come up for a little drinkie?"

Pause.

Oh, don't worry, nothing happened, because no kept saying no and yes kept saying yes and maybe kept saying maybe and doggie—even he couldn't stop peeing long enough to say anything else worthwhile to add to the conversations.

Pause.

Men! I hate them! Those mother-fuckers! You know why, kids? You really wanna know why! Because they have fucked me up, that's why! Ever since I was—so high—*Falls down.*

She looks off.

What do you mean—"shut up?" Shut up yourself, mother-fucker!

Front.

Did you hear that, kids? They won't let me express myself! I am constantly censored around here! They all live in fear around here! I don't know why, but even I, magical me, used to be that way—

fearful, fearful! But not anymore! I, right here and now, solemnly declare myself FREE! *Pause.* Look at me, just take a good look at me! Do I look afraid? Well—tell me! What do you see? *Pause.* I heard you! That wasn't nice—what you said. You take that back or I won't go on with my story!

Pause.

I was born . . . in the year of magic . . . to create magic wherever I go. That is all you shall know . . . and all you need to know. I was a star when I was a child. Millions saw in me the pure untouched innocence that they had somehow thought lost forever from the world . . . shinning beautifully, brilliantly . . . from out my eyes . . . my two baby blue eyes!

Pause.

Yes. I was a child star. Do you know what that means? You—. Do you know anything at all? What's on your mind? I mean, is there any magic at all in your heads—right now? What's in 'em? Oh, don't tell me—I know! Filth! Filth and fear and—and—

Magic spotlights out.

—and I am alone! No, you don't have to tell me—I know—I am all alone! Nevertheless, I shall go on . . . on with my story . . . and why? Why go on? Because the moral is—just that! Just that you have to go on! Alone and—it don't matter—because—because what does matter is—is—

She seems to draw a blank . . . then.

Cock-sucking! The contest! Oh, yes! Oh, dear God, I am so dumb about dates! Umm—let's see—that was on Thursday, January 7th—oh, 1760. Now on Friday morning, January, January the 8th—they turned on the TV and there he was—President Whats-His-Name! And President Whats-His-Name was looking kinda grim, kids. He was saying that the Russians were ahead by an inch and that from now on everybody would have to tighten their belts to make up for the difference. . . . Well, so everybody got out of bed and put on their clothes and tightened their belts a little and then everybody agreed for once that it certainly did make a lot of difference and they would certainly vote for him next year in Delaware. President-You-Know. Well, the next year in Delaware there they all were and sure enough of themselves were they that they all agreed that a year had certainly passed and weren't they silly? Well, the next step was they all had to agree that not only were they silly but—but—but that they were crazy.

Pause.

Crazy! I wish—I wish you kids . . . don't ever get like—like the people in this story—like—crazy!

Pause.

"Yes, yes, I'm crazy," the yes man said. "No, no, I'm crazy," the no man said. "Hey, you guys, maybe—maybe I'm crazy," the maybe girl said . . .

Pause.

Maybe!

Pause.

And the dog, too! Yes, he peed like crazy and wagged his ass like crazy because, you see, he didn't want to be left out, you can't blame him, left out of the craziness craze! And the Russians and Americans —all of 'em—they finally came out with a statement—at last—the cock-suckers finally came out with a signed statement at the end of which they all agreed—

Pause.

Oh—it was very long, with lots and lots of difficult words, words too big for you, my babies, to understand fully—but at the end of it, in very fine, very tiny printing were the words . . . "Yes. We are crazy, too."

Laughs triumphant.

Oh, well, of course, they thought that by that time nobody would even bother to read it that far down except—I did! Me! Your Magic Time Magic Lady . . . I did! I swear! You'll all just have to take my word for it, honey, those words were there, they really were, actually admitted it! They're all fucking crazy, all of them, I swear. And to think, at last, they actually admitted it! They know they are—!

Pause.

But do you know you are crazy, Magic Lady?

Pause.

No!
> *Pause.*

Yes!
> *Pause.*

Maybe . . . !
> *Pause.*

Ahh, the whole world is . . . *Looks out.* . . . waiting for you, babies . . . ! The whole world waits for you . . . to grow up . . . ! Yes! That's the moral . . . it is so important . . . I can't tell you how important it is—for you to grow up—clean . . . and—and brush your teeth religiously . . . yes, religion is also important because—you're hope . . . ! Yes! Yes! Our children are our only hope . . . aren't they? Aren't they?
> *Pause.*

Children . . . don't you ever lose your hope! Never ever lose it! Forget everything else . . . take away—throw away everything else—nothing matters—except hope . . . and there is no maybe about that.
> *Pause.*

Yes. This is your Magic Lady saying . . . that's all . . . for now! Magic Time is all over . . .
> *Bright smile.*

Nighty night . . . ! Goodnighty night, my children . . . !
> *Lights dim as she staggers out.*

CURTAIN

Family, Family

SALLY ORDWAY

FAMILY, FAMILY was seen at the Joseph Jefferson Theatre, 11 East 29th Street, New York City, in May, 1973, as part of a revue by the Westbeth Playwrights Feminist Collective. The production was directed by Cathy Roskam and the company included Lois Beckett, Jane Burch, Kristen Christopher, Richard Darrow, Norman Thomas Marshall and William Perley.

Other production: Westbeth Cabaret, February, 1971, directed by Marjorie Melnick.

Approximate playing time: 15 minutes

A bare stage. The action in the play should move swiftly and smoothly. Whatever furniture and props are used should be basic and serve multiple purposes. The ANNOUNCER *comes forward. She is a woman and plays the extra male roles in the play. Two men and two women are walking in a circle.*

FAMILY, FAMILY

ANNOUNCER: This is the nuclear family. *The* FAMILY *breaks from the circle as she introduces them. Actors play the female roles and actresses play the male roles. The father, the mother, the son, the daughter. Each actor steps forward as called.*

MARGARET (THE DAUGHTER): Nuclear?

SON: That's a bomb. You don't know anything. Stupid girl. Warfare, nuclear warfare. Don't you ever read the papers?

MOTHER: Don't pick on your sister. *The* MOTHER *sweeps and picks up throughout the play.*

ANNOUNCER: The American family in 1900 was considered very stable, the backbone of the country.

MARGARET: *pointing at her brother.* He's got the wishbone, Mama.

MOTHER: Let him have it, Margaret. He's a growing boy.

MARGARET: But he always gets it.

FATHER: Don't whine, Margaret. It's not ladylike.

SON: I'm going to be a nuclear physicist when I grow up.

MARGARET: And make nuclear warfare, I suppose. I hate warfare. Don't you hate warfare, Mama?

MOTHER: I've learned to live with it, Margaret. You must too.

FATHER: *swatting the* MOTHER *on the behind.* You're a good wife, Flo.

MARGARET: *to* SON. Ted, let me play with your erector set.

SON: *playing with it*. Go play dolls. Girls don't build things. You're such a dummy.

FATHER *begins dragging* SON *to playpen.*

MOTHER: *to* FATHER. Why are you so competitive, Charlie? They're just babies.

FATHER: So? We'll see which one gets the teddy bear first.

MOTHER: It's not fair. He's two years older.

FATHER: That's all right. O.K. now, at opposite ends of the playpen. Teddy bear in the middle. I'm betting on the boy.

They place the children in opposite corners on the imaginary playpen with the bear in the middle.

MOTHER: I don't believe in this.

FATHER: Bet on the girl. That'll balance it. *The children begin to move.* Here they go now. Come on tiger. Ted, the tiger. Get that Teddybear, Ted.

MOTHER: *giving up*. Oh well. Go, Margaret. MARGARET *closes in on the bear*. Oh, she's going.

FATHER: Come on, Ted. You're the man. Don't let your sister beat you!

MOTHER: *excited*. Oh, she's got it! She's got it!

FATHER: *harsh*. Get it back from her, Ted. You're stronger.

TED *tugs at the bear, but* MARGARET *gets a trick punch in and topples him.*

MOTHER: I think you'll have to say that Margaret won that round, Charlie.

FATHER: *disgruntled.* Well, girls develop faster than boys. Everybody knows that. But in the end . . .

MARGARET: Now can I play with your erector set, Ted?

SON: No. *Pushes her over.* Girls don't build things.

The FATHER *sits down with* TED *at the erector set.*

FATHER: That's right son. This erector set is the essence of a man's life. To build, to conquer.

MARGARET: Daddy, I'd like to be a doctor.

FATHER: Don't be silly, Margaret. Practice the piano.

MARGARET: *at the piano.* I hate the piano. I hate scales. I hate chords. *to* MOTHER. Can I have some ice cream?

MOTHER: No, it'll spoil your supper.

FATHER: Your daddy works hard at the store so you can take piano lessons and be accomplished.

MOTHER: If you practice one hour a day, you'll get beyond scales and chords.

FATHER: You practice, Margaret. It's a very attractive thing—a girl playing the piano. You'll get a lot of boyfriends that way when you're older. FATHER *leaves the scene.*

MARGARET: *to* TED *as she belches.* I beat you. I beat you!

SON: *belches.* No, you didn't.

MARGARET: Mine was louder.

SON: Was not.

MARGARET: Was too. MOTHER *comes in.*

MOTHER: Children, stop that! When your father's away you forget your manners. Margaret, try to behave like a lady. Ladies don't belch.

SON: Can I have another helping of dessert?

MOTHER: Yes. *Gives it to him.*

MARGARET: Can I?

MOTHER: No. Little girls are not supposed to be piggy. Remember the story I told you about the princess who ate like a bird and married the handsome prince.

MARGARET: I'd rather have a piece of cake. I would like to eat all the cakes and pies in the world.

The SON *fades out of the next scene.*

MOTHER: *to* MARGARET. You're getting to be quite a grown-up young lady now.

MARGARET: Then why can't I go to the movies on Saturday nights like Ted?

FATHER: You're a girl.

MARGARET: I made two A's and Ted only makes C's, but he gets to do everything and stay out later than I do.

MOTHER: It's not a question of grades.

FATHER: Lots of girls make the best grades at your age, but later it's the men who become the geniuses. The girls become the wives and mothers. Remember that.

MARGARET: What about George Eliot?

FATHER: *George* Eliot? Must be a man.

FATHER *leaves. A new scene.*

MOTHER: Dancing makes you graceful. All girls your age should know how to dance.

MARGARET: What about boys?

MOTHER: There'll be boys at the dancing class.

A BOY *comes into the scene.*

BOY: *to* MARGARET. Hello. I'm Earnest.

MARGARET: I'm Margaret.

They begin to dance.

BOY: You've put in an extra step.

MARGARET: Oh, I'm sorry. *A beat.*

BOY: Now, you're trying to lead me.

MARGARET: I hate these classes. My mother made me take them.

BOY: Don't grip so hard. My mother wants me to be popular with girls. That's why I have to take them. Will you vote for me for class president next month?

The BOY *leaves the scene.* MARGARET *turns to* MOTHER *who starts to turn up her hem.*

MOTHER: This is a lovely dress. You'll be the belle of the ball. But I wish you'd lose a few inches in your waistline. You could do exercises.

MARGARET: I feel awkward at dances. I don't know what to say to boys.

MOTHER: Just find out what the boy likes and talk about that. Boys love a good listener.

MARGARET: Some of them are so dumb.

MOTHER: Well, don't let them know you think you're smarter than they are. That's the first rule.

FATHER: *coming into the scene.* And don't talk about George Eliot.

MARGARET *picks up a book and begins reading it.*

FATHER: What are you reading now?

MARGARET: A biography of George Sand. She was a famous writer in nineteenth century Paris.

FATHER: She? Another George. All you know are Georges.

The scene changes to a drive-in movie.

MARGARET: George, stop. You're getting popcorn in my hair.

GEORGE: I'm sorry.

GEORGE: It was o.k. I liked him.

MARGARET: I didn't. He treated her shamefully.

GEORGE: She got what she deserved.

MARGARET: He treated her with contempt. Like he didn't think of her as a human being. So men have a monopoly on humanity like the telephone company has on communications?

GEORGE: Look, she was just a neurotic female. She was nuts.

MARGARET: Just because she wanted to do something out of the ordinary. To be herself. To be creative.

GEORGE: She should have stayed home and taken care of the kids. Look, I don't want to talk about the dumb movie. Let me touch your breast. I have to get the car home in 30 minutes.

New scene.

MOTHER: Are you going with George to the dance?

MARGARET: We broke up last night.

MOTHER: I'm sorry. He was a nice boy.

MARGARET: He was a shit. Is there any pie left?

MOTHER: I don't like that word. You're gaining weight. You should go on a diet.

MARGARET: I don't know what to do. I want to eat all the pies and cakes in the world. *Turning to* BOB. All right Bob, you can touch my breast. And I'll go out on a late date with you even if you are going steady with Sandra.

BOB: Would you like a hamburger?

MARGARET: Yes. With lettuce and tomato and cheese and a side order of french fries.

MARGARET: *turning to* MOTHER. I cleaned up my room, Mama.

MOTHER: I wish you'd go on a diet, Margaret.

MARGARET: I did, Mama. I ate bananas and skim milk for a whole week.

FATHER: Why can't you be like your brother, Margaret? He's president of his class this year and on the basketball team.

MARGARET: I haven't won any of my competitions.

A new boy comes in.

JOE: Can you go out with me after I take Jane home from the dance tonight, Margaret? Bob told me to call you.

JOE *leaves.*

MARGARET: Mother, you said everyone would love me if I was a good little girl, if I cleaned up my room and kept my dresses clean.

MOTHER: I found a high protein diet in the Ladies Home Journal.

MARGARET: College will be better. Everybody will be more mature. They'll appreciate me for who I am.

MOTHER: I'm glad you're going to a girl's school. I liked the atmosphere there the first time I saw it. I love colonial architecture. I hope you'll prepare for a teaching career. And try to lose some of that weight.

MARGARET: And my last year in college I lost weight.

MOTHER: I wish you'd meet a nice young man and get married.

HARRY *comes in.*

HARRY: *on top of* MARGARET. You taste good. Like lemon merangue pie.

MARGARET: You have such contempt for me.

HARRY: I don't.

MARGARET: You do. It's the way you were brought up. The way I was brought up. Our roles.

HARRY: I have respect for you.

MARGARET: How could you have respect for me?

HARRY: I thought it was respect.

MARGARET: I can't marry you, Harry. You only care about my tits. I'm a female who is human, not a human who is female. *Angry.* Oh Christ! I've had it. I won't say another line of this damn thing!

MOTHER: I'm with you, (ACTOR'S NAME). I hate saying my lines.

SON: I love saying mine.

MOTHER: Dyke!

MARGARET: She's loaded it on your side. Families aren't like this.

OTHER MAN: (ANNOUNCER, GEORGE, HARRY) That's not true. I come from a family just like this in Lima, Ohio.

FATHER: You can't just stop the play like this.

MARGARET: Why not? I'm not getting paid for this shit.

SON: You had a damn good part.

MARGARET: In drag.

OTHER MAN: Look, she's right, you know. You can't just leave Margaret's life unfinished like that. You should at least let the audience know what happened.

MARGARET: All right.

SON: I'll tell it. You're too hostile. *to the audience.* Margaret got away from her family. She made something of herself. Eventually, she became quite a well-known shrink specializing in the psyches of women. She never married, but had several interesting lovers, men and women.

MARGARET: *to audience.* The old Cinderella story, right? But that's not what happened at all. What the hell! Think what you want. I'm leaving.

MOTHER: Me too.

SON: They can't take the turn-around. It's our roles, the way we've been taught. It isn't fair to either one of us now, is it?

Lights fade and come up on another nuclear family beginning the play again.

ANNOUNCER: This is the nuclear family. They live in middle America. The father, the mother, the son, the daughter.

BLACKOUT

Coffee Stand

SHARON THIE

> COFFEE STAND was seen at the Dove Company, 346 West 20th Street, New York City, in April, 1972. The production was directed by Donald Kvares and featured the following actors:

> SELMA . . . . Marcia Mohr
> JIM . . . . Harold Herbstman
> RONNIE . . . . Duane Tucker

> *Approximate playing time: 45 minutes*

The scene is a coffee stand on a city street. The counter opens out on the sidewalk. A green and white striped awning above it reads "Selma's Coffee and Sandwiches Stand." There are mustard, ketchup, relish, napkins, straws, and candies on the counter. Selma is about fifty, big, strong, healthy, forceful. She may have an accent, but it is not French. Jim is about thirty-five, elegant, handsome, very well-dressed and extremely polite. Ronnie is a ragged but good-spirited old man. Selma stands behind her counter as Jim approaches hurriedly.

JIM: One container of black coffee, please.

SELMA: How many sugars?

JIM: No sugar, please.

SELMA: *warmly.* By black do you mean no cream at all?

JIM: *smiling.* No, no cream at all. Just black coffee, please.

SELMA: *with increasing warmth and concern for Jim.* You know, cream in your coffee is not a bad habit. It helps to balance all the acid, the caffein.

JIM: *with polite interest.* Balance the acid? Hm. I'll take it black, please.

SELMA: The Indians, the Indian Indians, you know, always drink cream in their tea for that reason. It helps to balance the acid for them.

JIM: *with polite admiration.* You know a great deal about coffee and tea.

SELMA: People say I have a natural gift.

JIM: You must. *With slight impatience.* I'll take black coffee, please.

SELMA: In Italy they put hot milk in coffee. Call it Capuccino.

JIM: My heavens. You do know a plethora of details.

SELMA: I have to study the whole subject. I have to concentrate when I work.

JIM: You must. I'll take the black coffee, please.

SELMA: You've heard of Irish Coffee, haven't you? That has your pure whipped cream dropped on the top.

JIM: *smiling, he drops his change on the counter in an elegant gesture of despair.* I want black coffee. Just one black coffee, please.

SELMA: *a word that is like an embrace by her; she will always say it with great compassion and warmth.* Sure.

JIM: *seeing that she has not moved.* Could you get me one container, please?

SELMA: *not moving.* Sure.

JIM: *pointing to his watch.* I'm in a terrible hurry.

SELMA: Oh, sure.

JIM: I'm already ten minutes late.

SELMA: *overwhelmed with compassion; she grasps his arm.* Oh sure.

JIM: You're very kind. But my jacket—wrinkles very easily.

SELMA: *letting go.* Oh, your jacket. Oh, sure.

JIM: I have to meet a very important man. It's a business appointment. *Gestures.* Uptown.

SELMA: *helping him brush his jacket.* Sure. And your jacket. Oh, sure.

JIM: I know I must sound terribly impatient. But could you get me my container of black coffee, please?

SELMA: *smiling brightly.* Sure.

JIM: When I'm late like this, I feel a little bit insane.

SELMA: You don't look insane.

JIM: Thank you.

SELMA: Sure. You don't look insane at all. *Looks in his eyes.* You're very becoming.

JIM: Thank you.

SELMA: I don't say that to everyone, you know.

JIM: Well, thank you.

SELMA: You think I say that to all the men, don't you?

JIM: No, I don't think that at all.

SELMA: You think I want you to buy more coffee, don't you?

JIM: No, I don't. Really I don't.

SELMA: You're the first man I ever called becoming in my life.

JIM: Thank you. I'll remember that. *Looking at his watch.* Oh, I'm very late.

SELMA: I want to show you something. *Taking his hand in hers.* Here.

JIM: *pulling his hand away from her.* No, really, thank you, but I haven't got time!

SELMA: This will just take a minute.

JIM: I haven't got a minute now, **really**.

SELMA: That's not true. When you haven't got a minute, you're dead.

JIM: I almost feel like you are trying to make me late, miss.

SELMA: **Selma.**

COFFEE STAND

JIM: Selma.

SELMA: I am Selma, and you are the first man that I have ever called becoming in my life.

JIM: Selma, could I have my coffee now, please?

SELMA: First, I want you to give me your hand.

JIM: If I give you my hand I am going to be late.

SELMA: Give me your hand!

JIM: *scooping his change up off the counter.* Forget the coffee.

SELMA: *grabbing his hand.* Aha! Now. *Sensuously.* I want you to feel my hand. I want you to feel the skin on my hand. I want you to feel your skin against mine.

JIM: *weakly.* I really don't want to.

SELMA: It excites you, doesn't it?

JIM: No.

SELMA: My skin is like water in a cold stream. My skin is like new milk at twilight on a farm. My skin is like petals of roses by a wellhouse.

JIM: No.

SELMA: I am a woman with beautiful skin.

JIM: No, you're not. You really are not.

SELMA: And it arouses you, doesn't it?

JIM: No.

SELMA: Yes. You are almost beyond control.

JIM: Will you stop this!

SELMA: And you desire my flesh.

JIM: I don't even like it. Really.

SELMA: But I am too beautiful for you. I am too beautiful for all men. Even you.

JIM: Please give me my hand back, will you? All I wanted was my coffee. You're making me late.

SELMA: Ssh.

JIM: Ssh?

SELMA: Be quiet. Be still.

JIM: *whispering.* Please!

SELMA: *a glassy look entering her eyes.* I want to tell you something. We are together in the royal court of France.

JIM: We're not.

SELMA: Yes. Be still. It's you and I.

JIM: *trying to pull his hand away, but politely, and casting desperate, embarrassed glances around him.* Stop this!

SELMA: We are together in the royal court of France. *Ronnie approaches.*

SELMA: And I, at this point in the history of nations, I am the most desired of women. I am the most desired woman in the land.

RONNIE: Hey, Selma?

SELMA: Throughout France, men want me, they dream about me. At the mention of my name, their eyes glow with a special look and their faces flush with a special heat. Because every man in France has heard of me, has agreed that my beauty is unsurpassed, has whispered that my sexual power is unique.

JIM: *almost crying now.* Oh, no. . . .

SELMA: When blacksmiths are working or eating lunch at their benches, it is me they feel in their hands. When wealthy men are drinking and smoking, it is my body they see in their eyes. When scholars and artists are thinking, creating, it is my beauty that obsesses their minds.

RONNIE: Hey! Selma!

SELMA: And when strong men, virile men, when great lovers are alone at night, alone in their beds, they cannot think of other women. It is me who consumes them in dreams of lust.

JIM: Oh, stop this, stop it, please!

SELMA: And I, at this point in the history of nations, I am also the queen of France.

RONNIE: You gettin' too good to say hello to me or sumpin', Selma?

SELMA: One night I plan a private party at my palace. And I invite one hundred chosen men. Nobles, soldiers, artists and scholars, the most beautiful and virile, the most desirable men in the land.

JIM: If you don't let my hand go—I think I may bite you.

SELMA: I have promised them a sight they would die for, a thrill they have dreamed of, alone at night, or when other women are in their arms. I have promised them a vision they are breathless just imagining. I have promised them that I, the queen of France, will undress.

RONNIE: *moving closer to hear her better.* Hey—Selma. Are you gonna strip?

SELMA: *ignoring him still.* I am going to arouse my chosen men with the slow and tempting revelation of my body. I am going to incite them with my movements and my dancing. I am going to make them burn to feel me, to feel my skin, and to come inside.

JIM: Please let me go. I feel a little sick now.

SELMA: But the queen of France does not strip. The queen of France undresses. No, the queen of France disrobes.

RONNIE: You gonna do it or yap about it, Selma? Huh?

SELMA: On my special night, the chosen gather in my throne room. They are exquisitely dressed, they drink and smoke, they talk, they gesture, they strike elegant poses, but there is one and only one thing in their minds.

JIM: *his hand remaining in Selma's, his head dropping down on his arm.* I'm sick to my stomach. Someone should stop this. . . .

SELMA: Every man in the room knows I am coming. They steal quick little glances at the doorway. And every one of them is fantastically aroused.

RONNIE: You never change. You're all talk, Selma. You're always nothin' but yap, yap, yap, yap.

SELMA: Suddenly, there is a fanfare of music. *Salome—Dance of the Seven Veils,* by Richard Strauss *begins to play under.* And a hush grips every man in the room. They stop in the middle of sentences and gestures. And they turn, each one breathless, to my special door.

The music builds, it swells, it crescendoes. The door swings slowly open and I, the queen of France, am standing there. I look incredibly beautiful. I am queen, I am woman, I am empire, I am France. I wear a dress of diamond and velvet. My breasts are pushed high and tight above the edge.

RONNIE: *obviously fascinated, moving very close now.* Oh, yeah?

SELMA: My face and hair are exquisite. They are beautiful. And my skin is like cream, like snow against velvet. My skin is irridescent. It shimmers and swells.

RONNIE: *becoming aroused.* Yeah, Selma. I like it when it swells.

SELMA: Two chosen courtiers meet me at my doorway. They take me by my hands and I walk into the room. I smile coyly. I turn so that every man can see me. I can feel their driving desire for my body. I can feel their desperate longing for me.

RONNIE: Move a little, Selma. That'll get 'em hotter.

SELMA: But I am supreme and confident. I arch my back. I stand motionless. And I smile.

The music becomes slow, sensual, insistent. And my two courtiers unbutton my dress. Slowly, and with reverence, they remove the top of it. I can hear the men gasp very quietly at what they see.

RONNIE: *with one of his hands on his fly.* Go, Selma, go, Selma, go.

SELMA: My breasts are white and round and full. My nipples are covered with diamonds and rubies. Just at the tip, and my breasts swell out. With my hands I begin to caress them. I sway from side to side. I am smiling. I play with my nipples. I can hear the men breathing. I can feel every man in the room getting tight.

JIM: *weakly, with his head down.* Stop.

RONNIE: *to Jim.* You shut up.

SELMA: "What exquisite breasts," the men whisper to each other. "I must touch them, I must have them in my mouth." I begin to dance. My body traces the motions of love. And I, now I am excited too.

My courtiers come to me. They kneel before me. And slowly and reverently they unbutton my skirt. They hold it around me for a moment. I can see that every man is swelling with desire. I can feel every member in the room reach out to me.

Suddenly, the courtiers whisk my skirt away from me. And I, the queen of France, am standing there.

RONNIE: *with both hands over his fly now, turning his back.* That's my Selma! Go, oh Selma, go!

SELMA: "Exquisite hips," the men whisper to each other. "Divine stomach," one of them gasps. "Her navel was formed for my tongue," says another. And every man in the room agrees.

My heaven is covered with a shield of diamonds. And one ruby, one smouldering ruby, is set into me, at the top of my sky. Every man in the room wants that ruby, wants it so badly that he's absolutely tight.

Ronnie makes aroused sounds, his back turned, appearing to masturbate.

SELMA: My courtiers come to me. They seize the diamonds from the tips of my nipples. I smile coyly at both of them. And then I allow them to taste.

The men are highly agitated. They are wild. They are ardent. But I smile coyly, and my smile says, "Control."

I remain supreme and confident. Gently, I take my nipples from my courtiers. And I walk about the room, among my men. "See my breasts," I say to one of them. "See how beautiful they are when they've been loved?"

"Beautiful," he says. "Oh, I want them, I want them."

"Do you?" I say, and I arch my back and smile.

I walk very close to him. He is seated before me. And I place one nipple at the edge of his lips. He is driven insane with desire. But he waits for my word, because my smile tells him, "Control." I move my nipple back and forth in front of his mouth, until he cannot bear it any longer. Then I smile down at him, and I say to him, "You may taste." He takes my breast full in his mouth. He is in ecstasy.

"Drink me, drink me," I say to him. And he drinks from my breast so deeply that it answers the thirst he has felt all his life. After a few moments, I pull away from him. It is painful for him, and I know it is painful, but I smile coyly and I touch his lips, and I say to him, "There now, I must move on."

I turn to the other men in the room and I say, "See my nipples, see how beautiful my nipples are in love?"

And I stop by a dark, strong man, and I smile down at him and I tell him he may suck. He does so, slowly and with great pleasure, and I say to the others, "Look, gentlemen, look at my nipples, how full and hard now. I am becoming aroused."

All the men gasp, and I say, "I would like to come now." I walk to another man. *Tapping Jim.* That man is you.

I stand in front of you, but you look away from me. You tap your fingers. You try to look bored. You love me too much to seem aroused like the others. But I know you, you are *not* bored, no, inside you, you *bleed*.

"A little pussy?" I say, smiling down at you. But you do not answer. You tap your fingers and try with all your might to look bored.

"Just a little pussy? Come love, I know you want it." I take your head and I turn your lips to *me*.

I say, "Take my diamonds, take the ruby from my slit, love. I know you want it." At long last, you look up.

Your eyes are dark and wet and shining. They are tired but full of desire for me. Your eyes are very proud yet yearning. I love you, I love your desire for me. I take your head very firmly in my hands. I tell you to take the diamonds from my pussy.

"Take them, love. I know you want to see me."

Finally your hands reach up to me and you lift away my little shield of diamonds so that I, the queen of France, am standing there. While the other men watch, I sway back and forth before you. I put my pussy very close to your lips. I know you can see me and smell me and that you want me. Finally I stop, I am right against your lips **now.**

I say, "Take the ruby from my slit, love. Come, love, take it from me." You do, as my body ignites with sensations. You grasp me by my thighs now. You take me in your mouth.

I tell you to drink me. "Drink all of me, love. I am the answer, I am the answer to your life."

My two courtiers come to me. They lift me above you. They lift me above your head, like a swan. My back arched, my arms out, I smile at the men in the room below me. I am the queen of France . . . and a swan.

Then each courtier takes a nipple in his lips and you stand up to me. You take me in your mouth. I feel the high moment. It is very near now. I tell all the men to look at me. I am coming. And I know that when I do, all men will come. Then you grasp me and drink more deeply than ever, and I scream in a high, long moment of ecstasy, as every man in the room . . . replies. *The music stops.*

Ronnie makes sounds of coming.

SELMA: After awhile, the courtiers lower me to the floor again. I kiss your lips. Then I walk out of the room.

RONNIE: *turning to her, his eyes alive with admiration.* Hey, Selma —

SELMA: *as though seeing him for the first time.* What are you doing on my sidewalk? Get off.

JIM: *his head down.* Oh, god. I'm so sick. And I'm so late.

SELMA: *tenderly lifting his head.* Sure. And you seem to be very upset.

COFFEE STAND

JIM: *coming to himself, straightening up, brushing his jacket.* No, I'll be fine now. Thank you so much for your — story. Listen, you didn't forget my coffee, did you?

SELMA: Sure. But you're upset now. *Getting a cup of tea.* You should have a cup of tea.

RONNIE: I'll take a cup of coffee, Selma.

SELMA: Get off my sidewalk. Get off!

JIM: Thank you, but I really *don't* have time for tea now.

SELMA: Sure. *Hands him the cup of tea.* Milk and sugar? Sure.

JIM: No sugar, thank you. Just cream.

SELMA: *handling him a cream pitcher.* Sure. You shouldn't have cream with tea. Just milk.

RONNIE: I could stand a cup of coffee, Selma. It's been three days since I ate.

SELMA: Go eat one of your women. But get off my sidewalk, Ronnie. Get off! *To* JIM. This is a very big city, you know. It has a thousand sidewalks. A million of them. But my friend there doesn't think other sidewalks are good enough. Not for old Ronnie. He has to stand on mine.

JIM: *smiling tentatively at* RONNIE. He's a friend of yours?

SELMA: He's my husband. My former.

JIM: Oh. Are you — separated?

SELMA: *laughing.* Separated? We're done. *Looking fondly at* JIM. You want a sandwich with your tea, don't you? Sure.

JIM: *gulping tea.* No, thank you, I really have to *go.*

SELMA: Sure. You're hungry. That's why you're upset. Sure.

RONNIE: You're feeding him, Selma. You could give me a cup of coffee.

SELMA: Ronnie, I'm telling you to get off my sidewalk. *Leaning over the counter toward him.* I'm telling you to get off my sidewalk or else.

RONNIE: Else what, Selma? I'm starving, I tell ya'.

SELMA: Else, Ronnie, I'm gonna make you bleed. *To* JIM. Sure. You want your hamburger. Your fresh burger. I get your fresh meat in here every day.

JIM: Look, I should be meeting a man this minute. I'm supposed to be in his office right now.

SELMA: Sure. *Starting sandwich.* You want your hamburger rare? Medium? *Looking up at him.* Well-done?

JIM: I can't stand being late. I can't stand it.

SELMA: Sure. You want it on a bun.

JIM: But I feel like there's nothing I can do about it. Nothing. Because I'm always late. I'm late everywhere I go. My mother used to say I'd be late to my own funeral. I used to hear her say that to my sister. They'd be waiting for me, downstairs, while I was trying to get dressed. Then my sister would say, "But, Mom, he's making *us* late." And my mother would say, "He can't help it. He's like your uncle. He'll waste every day of his life being late."

COFFEE STAND

RONNIE: Free country, Selma. I can stand here if I want to.

SELMA: You don't believe me, do you, Ronnie? You're gonna stand on my sidewalk until I come and make you bleed.

JIM: Every day, when I get up in the morning, I say to myself, "I am going to be on time. Today I am going to do everything calmly. Calmly and simply. And I have got to be on time."

I walk toward the bathroom to brush my teeth. I check my little clock on the table. I see that I have an hour, an entire hour to get dressed. I pick up my dirty ashtray from the table. Nothing seems as dirty to me as an ashtray. So I take the ashtray along to the bathroom and I empty the ashes and I wash the ashtray out. I pick up my toothbrush and think of coffee. Coffee tastes so fantastic in the morning. I carry the ashtray and my toothbrush to the kitchen. While I'm fixing my coffee, I notice something sticky, butter or something, in the middle of the stove. I go for the dishrag. I see last night's dishes. I decide I can wash them while the coffee's cooking. But, in the middle of washing the dishes, I remember that I never put the coffee *on*. I decide to brush my teeth first after all. I go back to the bathroom. I leave my toothbrush in the kitchen. Then I see the rug that's by the bathtub. It's all matted and full of footprints. So I run some water and I throw it in the tub. The tub has rings around it, but I don't have time for *that* now. I should scrub it, I can't stand those dirty tub rings. But I can't scrub it now, because I have to wash the rug. I bend over to put some soap flakes in the bathtub. And then I feel an awful pain in my stomach. And I realize that I must take time to pee. But first I'd like to finish the coffee. And I have to get my toothbrush. And I ought to check the time.

SELMA: Sure. You want catsup. *Looking at* JIM. You want mustard?

JIM: And the next thing I know I am lying back in bed again. I am so tired that I cannot even move. I can hear the clock ticking on the table, and I can't stand the sound of it, I just cannot stand that tick. And I glance at it and I see that I have ten minutes to get dressed now. Then something inside of me, like two huge muscles, start fighting each other, and I'm tearing in two.

Then I know that today is like all the others . . . I know I can never get dressed in ten minutes. I know I can never stop smoking or get organized. And I want to give into it. I want to stay in bed and fail.

But I think of coffee and I walk out to the stove again. I stand there wishing I could cry or scream or pick up the stove and throw it at someone. Or have those horrible muscles inside of me cut out . . . or fall in love so being late wouldn't matter . . .

But then I think, "Who would love you, you're a failure. You've been up an hour and you haven't brushed your teeth yet. Now put some clothes on your miserable body. And find your toothbrush. And wash the bathtub out. And pee."

SELMA: Sure. Your burger's on the griddle now. Sure.

RONNIE: If she feeds you, sonny, it means she wants to screw you.

SELMA: This is the last time I'm warning you, Ronnie. Get off my sidewalk. You're a bum. And you stink.

JIM: You wouldn't mind rushing my sandwich, would you?

SELMA: Sure. I'm turning your burger over. And here's your mustard. And your bun still has to toast.

RONNIE: Selma don't really sell sandwiches, sonny. She runs a whore house. She'll make you screw her. That's a whore house. She's a whore.

SELMA: *taking a police club out from under the counter.* I mean it, Ronnie. This time I mean it.

JIM: Miss — Selma — that's a police club.

SELMA: *tenderly.* Sure. It was a present to me. Sure. *Leaving the coffee stand.* This time you're bleeding, Ronnie. This time you bleed.

JIM: You shouldn't leave my hamburger cooking. I want it rare — I like it very, very rare —

RONNIE: Free country. You old whore.

SELMA: *to* JIM. Sure. I'll have your burger in a minute. *Advancing on* RONNIE. Okay, Ronnie. I want to see if you can bleed.

RONNIE: *realizing that she means it.* Wait a minute, Selma. I'll go now. I was going.

The climax of the Salome music plays under.

SELMA: *grabbing him by the coat.* No, you're not, Ronnie. You're gonna bleed. *Hitting him with the club on the word "bleed".*

RONNIE: Stop it, Selma! I'm going. I love you.

SELMA: *hitting him on the word "bleed".* Bleed, Ronnie. I want to see if you can bleed. Can you bleed, Ronnie? Got it in you? Come on, bleed!

JIM: Miss — Selma — stop that! You shouldn't do that!

RONNIE: *falling to the sidewalk.* Stop it, Selma. I love you, I love you.

SELMA: *continuing to hit him on the word "bleed".* You don't know how to bleed, do you, Ronnie? Come on, try to bleed, Ronnie. For once in your stinking life you should bleed.

RONNIE: I love you, Selma.

SELMA: Bleed for me, Ronnie.

RONNIE: Selma —

SELMA: Bleed, Ronnie. Bleed. Bleed for me. Bleed!

The music stops.

SELMA *looks at* RONNIE *for a moment. He lies motionless on the sidewalk, his hands and arms wrapped around his head.* SELMA *walks calmly back to the coffee stand and carefully puts her police club away.*

SELMA: Sure. Your hamburger's done now. It's just rare enough.

JIM: *staring at her as she brings the sandwich to him.* I'm not really hungry now. Really I'm not.

SELMA: Sure. Eat it. It's good for you. Sure.

JIM: I'm sorry, but I —

SELMA: Sure: Eat it. It's good for you. Sure.

JIM: I —

SELMA: Sure. Take it in your hands now. *Placing the hamburger in* JIM'S *hands.* Sure. And eat it now. *Pushing his hands up to his mouth.* Eat it now. Sure.

JIM *forces himself to take a bite.*

COFFEE STAND

SELMA: Sure. Chew it up now. Sure.

JIM: *trying hard to swallow.* Um.

SELMA: Sure. It's fresh meat. It's good meat. Sure.

JIM: Um. It tastes — very good.

SELMA: Sure. Take another bite. Swallow. Sure.

JIM: *suddenly choking.* Ew!

SELMA: What's wrong?

JIM: I bit something.

SELMA: What?

JIM: *coughing food out in his hand.* A tissue. A knot of tissue that someone blew their nose in. It's bitter.

SELMA: No.

JIM: It's sour. *Coughing.* Oh, god. I feel terribly — sick.

SELMA: Sure. Keep eating it. Sure.

JIM: *Dropping the hamburger on the counter.* I can't. I have to vomit. I'm sick.

SELMA: *forcing the hamburger back in his hands.* Sure. Keep eating.

JIM: I can't. I have to vomit.

SELMA: *forcing it to his mouth.* Sure. Keep eating.

JIM: *dry heaves.* No, no, please —

SELMA: Sure. Eat it.

JIM: No, please —

SELMA: Sure. Eat it. It's good for you. Sure.

She continues to force it to JIM's *mouth as* RONNIE, *moaning, rolls a little on the sidewalk and lights dim to darkness.*

CURTAIN

1 Piece Smash

ARTHUR SAINER

1 PIECE SMASH was seen at the Open Space Theatre Experiment, 37 St. Mark's Place, New York City, in July, 1970. The production was directed by Victor Esbach, and performed by Sully Boyer.

Other production: WBGM-TV (as TIMECHECK), directed by Paul Boessing.

Approximate playing time: 15 minutes

A piece of crockery smashes against a wall. The theatre is dark except for the area of the wall. Focus on the wall for a time. No sounds, no people. At last the theatre is totally dark again.

Lights up on CRAYON *in a different part of the theatre.*

CRAYON: It's not a time to make plays. We can't afford not to make plays. This is an editorial, don't listen. This play won't win awards—tough shit. This is not a play—more tough shit.

Item: Police gun down Panthers. Item: Police gun down demonstrators. Item: No place to go. Warning: Don't listen to these words if you're from Jersey. Warning: If you're from Jersey you may be indicted as part of a conspiracy. Suggestion: Don't be from Jersey. Counter suggestion: Use your head. Counter suggestion plus one: Your gut.

Hot news: The words I speak to you were written for me. Illumination: Have seen fuzz lie on witness stand, no coaching necessary. As

I say these words, some of us are lying with our bodies. Some of us are lying with our silences, we do it all day long.

Report: Nobody wants to be a coward, everybody wants to be warm. Item: Con Edison is tearing up the sidewalk. They do it cheerfully. It's a public service. Item: Things can't go on this way. Vote for Warren W. Napalm, he brings it to you in a basket. Item: Don't get me started.

Blackout. Again a piece of crockery is smashed against the wall. Again we focus on the wall for a time, with the rest of the theatre dark.

Again CRAYON *is seen.*

CRAYON: Quote—"If you are reading this letter you will never see me again. If you are reading this letter you are reading it because I have died. — The question is whether or not my death has been in vain. The answer is yes."

The wall. Another piece of crockery smashes. Focus on the wall for a time.

CRAYON: "You can be a revolutionary but you still have to put gas in your car."

She said, "Pardon me, didn't I just step on your foot?" He said, "Yes." She said, "I thought that was you."

The answer is yes.

If we give pleasure, is that a direction?

"After a few days the war in Cambodia took on the appearance of the war in Vietnam."

After a few days in the Garden of Eden, Adam introduced the six-pack. Eve introduced the orgasm. Satan introduced the anger of God. Satan introduced God's infinite sadness.

Again the wall. No crockery. Focus on the wall for a time. CRAYON *smokes in silence. The wall. Silence. Focus on the wall for a time.*

CRAYON: From the team that gave you I.T.T., Watergate, the milk scandal, the wheat scandal, the record-breaking war and assorted benefits too numerous to mention, a special bonus—Billy Graham sweatsox.

The wall. Focus on the wall for a time.

CRAYON: Bulletin: Perhaps it's only your government tuning in.

The answer is yes.

"To the recollection of the wanton murder of an Isaac Babel or an Osip Mandelstam is added the knowledge that Andrei Sinyavsky, his health broken by torture, may not survive his seven-year prison term." After a few months in the Garden of Eden, the newlyweds got an eviction notice. It was time to split anyway, the neighborhood was getting rough.

If you have nothing to say, now's the time.

The wall. Focus on the wall for a time. CRAYON *smokes in silence. Focus on the wall for a time. Focus on the wall for a time.*

CRAYON: By the late Seventies, mass starvation is predicted.

CRAYON *smokes in silence.*

CRAYON: Item: The Panthers are bleeding. The Vietnamese are bleeding. The Israelies are bleeding. The Americans are bleeding. The Arabs are bleeding. The Czechs are bleeding. If you have nothing to say, now's the time. If you have nothing to say, now's the time.
The answer is yes. The answer is yes.

The wall. A succession of pieces of crockery go smashing against the wall — one, two, three, four. Then silence. Hold on the wall for a long time. A long time. The silent wall, the broken crockery. Then the houselights slowly come up.

CURTAIN

Living Room With 6 Oppressions

OSCAR MANDEL

LIVING ROOM WITH 6 OPPRESSIONS was seen at the Playwrights Workshop Club, 14 Cooper Square, New York City, in January, 1973. The production was directed by Craig Barish and featured the following actors:

MATTHEW AVAILABLE	Roderick Carter
NANNY	Judith Levitan
WORKER	Robert Barger
CAPITALIST	George Salerno
PUERTO RICAN	Juan De Aguerra
NEGRO	Ralph Campbell
INNOCENT BYSTANDER	Bruno Ragniacci
POLICEMAN	Ken Fuchs

Other production: Actors Experimental Unit, April, 1973, directed by Richard Viola.

© 1970 by Oscar Mandel

LIVING ROOM WITH 6 OPPRESSIONS first appeared in the Spring 1970 issue of *Drama & Theatre*. The definitive version was printed in Volume One of Oscar Mandel's *Collected Plays* (Unicorn Press, 1970). All uses of this play are strictly controlled by copyright. For information on rights, write to the author c/o Division of the Humanities, California Institute of Technology, Pasadena, California 91109.

Approximate playing time: 40 minutes

LIVING ROOM WITH 6 OPPRESIONS

The action takes place in Matthew Available's comfortable living room. One of its doors leads directly to the street, another one leads to the kitchen. Matthew wears a lounging robe.

MATTHEW: Sunday afternoon. Fair weather, my pulse regular, all my rhythms in order, my mind alert, informed and compassionate. *He sits down with a ledger and rings a little bell.* Nanny! NANNY *appears.*

NANNY: You rang, Mr. Matthew?

MATTHEW: Yes I did. Bring my coffee, will you? And half a muffin with cinnamon.

NANNY: It's all ready in the kitchen; I'll just heat the muffin a bit.

MATTHEW: Fine. Don't burn it, though. *Exit* NANNY. MATTHEW *turns to his ledger.* Let's see. Twenty-five dollars for the Cancer Society. Fifty for the Orphanage. Forty for the blind. Poor people. I'd rather be deaf, dumb, anything. Another twenty for the Greek refugees. Twenty-five, fifty, forty, twenty — that makes a hundred thirty-five. I should be able to do better. I'm a bachelor, damn it, and Nanny doesn't cost much. I'll slow down buying books and use the library instead. There's been another earthquake in Sicily, an invasion in Yemen, a massacre or two in Indonesia, and here I am with my steady pulse and my slippers. Come to think of it, I've got my shoes on. On a Sunday afternoon! Nanny! *Impatient.* Nanny!!

NANNY: *from the kitchen.* What now?

MATTHEW: Why haven't I got my slippers on?

NANNY: The muffin will burn if I go for your slippers now!

MATTHEW: All right, all right. *To himself.* Always ready with an excuse. *Enter* NANNY *with a tray.*

NANNY: I'll get your slippers in a minute, but I've got to look —

MATTHEW: Damn damn damn. I've told you a million times — damn! Look at that lump of sugar.

NANNY: Well? I'm looking.

MATTHEW: It's wet!

NANNY: A bit of coffee spilled into the saucer.

MATTHEW: I *know* a bit of coffee spilled into the saucer! And yet I've told you a million times to bring me the sugar in a bowl. Do you know what I mean? A bowl, a crystal bowl, the way it's done in every bloody civilized household on earth.

NANNY: But why? Always the same story! Why all the fuss? You've been taking two lumps in your coffee for the last twenty years, Mr. Matthew, and you were taking two lumps in your hot milk when you were four years old, so what's the use my carting in a bowl full of useless lumps of sugar?

MATTHEW: The use is that the sugar won't get soggy. I hope it's not too much to expect — two dry lumps of sugar picked up with a pair of sugar tongs. Now what? What's this? What's going on?

The entrance door is flung open, and the Worker rushes in, more on all fours than on his two feet. He is bloody, abject, emaciated and exhausted.

WORKER: Help me, hide me, he's going to kill me!

MATTHEW: Who? What? Who are you?

NANNY: Get out of here, this is Mr. Available's private house!

WORKER: I'll explain later — Mr. Available — I'm beggin' you — save me — have a heart — I'm an honest working man and the owner is after me, I smashed his machine.

NANNY: Well! I advise you —

MATTHEW: Shut up, Nanny! Here, give me your hand, here's a closet —

WORKER: Too late! Oh Jesus!

The Capitalist rushes in.

CAPITALIST: Where's the swine?

WORKER: Protect me!

MATTHEW: Now wait a minute!

NANNY: This is private property!

CAPITALIST: *I* am private property. Don't hide behind chairs, you slum-bum, I'll rip you to pieces, striker, machine-breaker, drunkard, collective bargainer —

MATTHEW: Now wait a minute! This man is under my protection.

CAPITALIST: Who are *you?*

MATTHEW: What do you mean? This is *my* house. Kindly take your capitalist hide out of here, skinflint, blood-sucker, gouger, golf-player.

WORKER: That's tellin' him.

CAPITALIST: Hold it, feller.

MATTHEW: Nanny, show the gentleman the door.

NANNY: I keep telling you to lock that door of ours, Mr. Matthew.

MATTHEW: Never. Let nobody say that he found Matthew Available's door locked in his face. Good day, sir.

CAPITALIST: Good day my pink toe. I'll have that bolshevik gangster in manacles before I leave the house. Out of my way!

MATTHEW: What did he do to you?

CAPITALIST: He smashed my machine.

WORKER: I smashed his machine.

NANNY: Why, look at him. He's so weak he couldn't smash an eggshell.

WORKER: I smashed it all the same, and I'll keep smashing it till I get a living wage.

CAPITALIST: Scum! Ten years in the clink is what you'll get! Come out of there! *To* MATTHEW. Let me go, or I'll slug you too!

MATTHEW: Stop bawling. You bloated oppressor, how much longer are you going to live off the work of the poor?

CAPITALIST: As long as I can, you bet your life. I've smashed six unions in my time. And I'm not bloated, I'm well fed.

NANNY: Oh the wicked man.

WORKER: It's off of us the likes of him feed their faces. Me and my starvin' wife and my three sick kids, and a paycheck that ain't enough to feed the flies in our stinking two rooms. I wish I'd have smashed *him* instead of his machine.

CAPITALIST: Open threats!

MATTHEW: I'll say. And I'm the man to execute them. *He takes a poker from the fireplace.* See this? Solid brass. Nanny, give me a hand. NANNY *grabs a monstrously abstract wooden sculpture.*

WORKER: Hit him!

CAPITALIST: Oh yeah? I'm not leaving without this anarchist in custody.

MATTHEW: Yes you are.

CAPITALIST: No I ain't.

NANNY: Yes you are.

CAPITALIST: Out of my way, granny, I'll have you both up for conspiracy.

MATTHEW: Get out!

CAPITALIST: Get out yourself!

MATTHEW: *To* NANNY. Hold him!

CAPITALIST: I'll knock your teeth into your windpipe.

WORKER: Hit him! Hit him! MATTHEW *hits the* CAPITALIST.

CAPITALIST: Ouch!

NANNY: Parasite! *She hits him too and lays him out flat.*

WORKER: That's the ticket! *He comes out from behind a chair and kicks the* CAPITALIST. I wish I was stronger.

MATTHEW: Sit down, my poor man. Nanny will give you something to eat. And I'll drag this carcass out.

CAPITALIST: *opens an eye.* What hit me?

NANNY: *shows him the sculpture.* Justice Unbound.

CAPITALIST: Damn. *He faints away.*

MATTHEW: Give me a hand, Nanny. All that blubber. *They drag the* CAPITALIST *outdoors.* So much for that. The world can stand a little improvement. How are you feeling, Mr. —?

WORKER: Smiggins. Josh Smiggins. And real grateful to the both of yous.

NANNY: I'll fix you something to eat, Mr. Smiggins. You look like you're about to become extinct.

WORKER: Gee, I'd appreciate a little something. Just anything will do, ma'am; I ain't used to much.

NANNY: Leave it to me. *She goes to the kitchen.*

MATTHEW: It's about time somebody stood up to these robbers.

WORKER: Without you I'd a been in jail by now, Mr. Available.

MATTHEW: Well, I did my best. I may be an intellectual, but you don't find *me* playing a harp in an ivory tower.

WORKER: Doin' what?

MATTHEW: I mean, refusing to fight.

WORKER: Refusin' to fight? You? Don't you believe it. That poker o' yours coulda laid out five of him. Boy, if I wasn't a wreck —

MATTHEW: Nanny! Hurry up!

NANNY: *within.* Coming, coming!

WORKER: I don't want to be no trouble to you.

MATTHEW: Trouble? I ought to apologize to you for living in ease and comfort while you — and your wife — and those poor children — God, it makes me choke —

WORKER: Me too. This sure is nice lodgins you got here. A reglar nest, bless you all. *Enter* NANNY *with a tray full of bread, butter, cold cuts and cheeses.*

WORKER: Oh gee, thanks, thanks a million. I'm so hungry, I can't hardly keep my head up.

MATTHEW: Heartbreaking. Here, eat, make yourself at home.

WORKER: Mmmm. Good.

MATTHEW: More butter, Mr. Smiggins?

WORKER: Good idea. What do you know! I'm feeling stronger already.

MATTHEW: *To* NANNY. It's a pleasure to watch him.

NANNY: Why don't I put something in a paper bag for your children, Mr. Smiggins?

WORKER: Gee, would you? They'll be real happy, the poor kids.

MATTHEW: Let's hope that your children will see a brighter future. No exploitation, a decent wage, a good education.

WORKER: *his mouth full.* You said it. Boy oh boy, do I feel better! Lemme wash this down with a cup of coffee, do you mind? Smells great. "Good to the last drop." Yes, sir, I'm gonna put the kids through college, right along with the board of directors, the jet set, Mr. Rockefeller, and everybody.

MATTHEW: Let them read Sophocles, study the sciences, hear chamber music.

WORKER: You bet. I'll see them at the top o' the heap if I ever get half a break at my lousy job. Gee, this here ham is the best I ever ett. Thanks for the bag, granny. *While eating, the* WORKER *has become remarkably stronger, larger, ruddier.*

MATTHEW: This meal has really propped you up, Mr. Smiggins. I hope today will mark a new beginning — and you know you can count on me. Well now, listen to this! *Music outside.*

WORKER: What's that?

MATTHEW: I don't know. Nanny, why don't you take a peek outside.

NANNY: I will. *She goes out.*

WORKER: Sure sounds foreign to me.

MATHEW: I think it's Puerto Rican.

WORKER: Oh yeah?

MATTHEW: Chamber music, Mr. Smiggins. I realize that this sounds a bit remote to you, but it's what your children will need. The best that civilization has to offer, once the bonds of slavery are broken, once men become true brothers. Go on, my friend, have another sandwich.

WORKER: I dunno. Them foreigners upset my appetite.

MATTHEW: I don't see why. *Nanny reappears.* Well, Nanny?

NANNY: It's the Virgin of Guadalupe's birthday, and they're all coming this way, bless 'em, dancing and banging on things.

WORKER: *roars.* I don't like foreigners!

MATTHEW: Mr. Smiggins! We're all Americans here. Remember the melting pot.

WORKER: *roars.* I don't like foreigners!

NANNY: *aside to* MATTHEW. We gave him too much to eat.

MATTHEW: Mr. Smiggins, all kinds of people went to the building of this nation — the English, the Poles, the Swedes, the Chinese, the Mexicans—

WORKER: *roars.* I don't like lousy foreigners! They grab our jobs for half pay and what do they do? They take a plane back home first chance they get, and jabbering away jabber jabber in their lingo that ain't even white. *At the door.* Cut out that noise! Jesus, lemme take a crack at them!

MATTHEW: Wait, hold it, hold it!

WORKER: Out o' my way! This place is for hundred percent Americans and union labor! I ain't gonna stand for no heathen celebrations!

MATTHEW: Nanny, help me!

WORKER: I'll moider em!

NANNY: Watch the gueridon!

MATTHEW: Mr. Smiggins!

The WORKER *has thrown* MATTHEW *off and flings himself into the street. Loud Latin music outside. Suddenly the music stops. Sounds of a fight, curses, trumpets blaring off-key. Then a Puerto Rican rushes into the house, more on all fours than on his two feet. He is mauled, enfeebled, astonished and terrified.*

PUERTO RICAN: Help me, hide me, Jesus Maria, he's going to kill me, the Yankee has gone mad!

MATTHEW: Close the door, Nanny, quick!

NANNY: Can I lock it, Mr. Matthew?

MATTHEW: Never! Here, sir, here, sit down, you're safe, believe me, we'll protect you. Here's a handkerchief.

PUERTO RICAN: Thank you, señor, thank you. Oh I can't breathe, I'm dying.

MATTHEW: *to* NANNY. Get him a glass of wine, hurry. Gently, my friend, you're not dying, you're only scared. My name is Matthew Available. You're safe under my roof, and I am going to give you all the help I can.

PUERTO RICAN: Mucho gusto. My name is José García. I don't even know what happened. It's the feast of the Virgen de Guadalupe today. *He crosses himself.* Thank you, señora, kind lady. *He drinks.* She is our holy guardian. We were singing and dancing. I was one of the men chosen to carry her on my shoulders.

NANNY: I don't see how you could carry a statue, Mr. García, you're so thin and weak I could break you in two by throwing a glance at you.

MATTHEW: Nanny!

PUERTO RICAN: There were six of us carrying her, señora, before that wild bull fell on us. Who was he, anyway? Why did he start knocking peaceful people down?

MATTHEW: Hm — I don't know. Lack of education, I'd guess.

PUERTO RICAN: I thought I saw him coming out of here.

MATTHEW and NANNY: Oh no.

PUERTO RICAN: We weren't doing anything wrong.

MATTHEW: I should say not. It's marvelous to see so many of you keeping faith with your traditions and beliefs. It's beautiful.

NANNY: Oh yes.

MATTHEW: Look at your history — Ponce de León — Sir Francis Drake — Morro Castle — Mr. García, I'm proud to have you as a guest in my house. Did you know that Puerto Rico had a sugar mill in 1548?

PUERTO RICAN: Wonderful.

MATTHEW: It was operated by oxen.

NANNY: Speaking of oxen, I think Mr. García would enjoy a ham and cheese sandwich.

PUERTO RICAN: Oh no. Please. You've both been too nice. The Virgin will bless you, but I'd better go now. *He tries.* I can't.

NANNY: I knew it.

MATTHEW: That does it. Bring some food, and plenty of coffee.

PUERTO RICAN: You shouldn't . . .

MATTHEW: Nonsense! On your way, Nanny.

NANNY: Good thing it's Sunday only once a week. *She goes.*

MATTHEW: Relax, Mr. García. If there's anything I can't abide, it's national prejudices. Imagine one people thinking itself better than another. I know you're not feeling well.

PUERTO RICAN: Oh, yes . . .

MATTHEW: No no, you're shivering.

PUERTO RICAN: A little, maybe. Nerves.

MATTHEW: We'll put you on your feet again. If only people could understand the idea of brotherhood, regardless of race, religion, nationality, and what not. I try my best as an individual. I contribute, I sympathize, I join, I fight — literally fight, you know — look at this bruise.

PUERTO RICAN: Caramba.

MATTHEW: Fighting a brutal capitalist, defending a poor workingman.

PUERTO RICAN: You mean the one who almost killed me?

MATTHEW: Maybe he was the one. I couldn't stop him, Mr. García.

PUERTO RICAN: You did your best, amigo.

THE SCENE

LA MAMA, E.T.C.

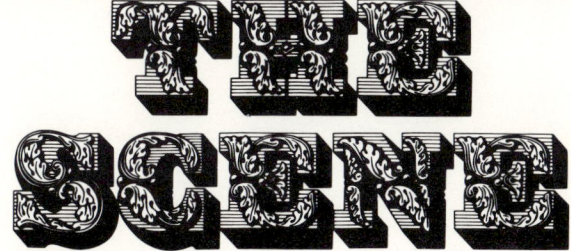

PHOTO ESSAY BY MICHAEL CAMPIONE

The Joseph Jefferson Theatre kicked off its season with an exciting 'Rip Van Winkle. Director Neil Flanagan makes costume adjustments, while Lucy Lee Flippen prepares to play Rip's wife. JJT artistic director Cathy Roskam **(above right)** looks quite happy. Also pleased are WPA's Harry Orzello, Dan Dietrich and Virginia Aquino; their Obie Award theatre continues to mount such groovy plays as Robert Patrick's 'Hippy As A Lark.' Another very . . .

... active group is Theatre 77 Rep, whose recent productions have included 'A' by Stanley Nelson (right), 'Old Folks' by Harvey Zuckerman (below left) and 'The New York Transit Authority' by Joseph Lazarus. Some theatres ...

... aren't where they used to be; the New York Theatre Ensemble now has fancier quarters but the old NYTE housed some memorable productions. Below Aurelia DeFelice and Beeson Carroll appear in Arthur Kopit's 'Conquest of Everest.' At right, Kopit adjusts Ms Felice's hemline. Among the . . .

... established resources of the OOB scene are Al Carmines, whose 'The Faggot' ran and ran, and Phebe's, still the chief after-hours spot for actors, directors and playwrights. And did you recognize the Face in Four Parts? It's Maurice Edwards of the Cubiclo.

MATTHEW: It takes time. Generations.

PUERTO RICAN: Centuries.

MATTHEW: Aeons.

PUERTO RICAN: Eternity?

MATTHEW: But I keep fighting. Decency. Human decency, you know; nothing startling or exceptional. Nanny! Damn her! Where's the food? How long are you going to keep us waiting?

NANNY: Coming, coming! *She enters with another tray.* This is the best I could whip together.

PUERTO RICAN: I'm —

MATTHEW: It's perfectly all right, Mr. García. Eat, get some strength, and pay no attention to us.

PUERTO RICAN: Delicious. My compliments, señora. I'm already feeling much better.

NANNY: Don't eat too fast.

MATTHEW: Café con leche?

PUERTO RICAN: *laughing.* Si, amigo. Muchas gracias. Oh yes, you're right, it's tough to be a small downtrodden people, Mr. —— ?

MATTHEW: Available. I know it must be.

PUERTO RICAN: What are we Latins next to you Yankees? Midgets. And besides, here in America we're second-class citizens. If it wasn't for a few decent nice people like you and the señora —

MATTHEW: Don't mention it.

The PUERTO RICAN *is beginning to look stronger.*

NANNY: You're beginning to look stronger, Mr. García.

PUERTO RICAN: Thanks to you both. I'll say a prayer for you. Oh look! Your door is moving. If it's that worker, I'll smash his face.

MATTHEW: Don't excite yourself, Mr. García. It was only the wind, I'm sure.

NANNY: I'm not so sure. Lookee.

In fact, the door has been opening slowly. On the floor we see the head of a Negro, followed by its body: dusty, shriveled, sweating and defeated.

NEGRO: Help, good people . . . *He speaks with an Oxonian accent.*

MATTHEW: *flings himself toward the door.* Come in, in God's name, come in, my brother!

NANNY: Another lunch coming up.

PUERTO RICAN: *glumly, to* NANNY. This is a relative? This?

NANNY: Oh no, Mr. García, only a visitor.

PUERTO RICAN: *indignant.* A visitor!

MATTHEW: *bending over the* NEGRO. What's the matter? Are you injured? Don't worry, you're safe in this house. Nanny, give me a hand, damn it!

NANNY: Sure, sure.

LIVING ROOM WITH 6 OPPRESSIONS

NEGRO: I can't speak . . . Whoever you are, if there's any pity left . . .

MATTHEW: Come on, let me help you get on your feet. *To* NANNY. Take the other arm. One, two, three! Here we are! To the leather chair. There now. Easy, easy. My God, he's bleeding in the neck.

PUERTO RICAN: *aside*. Troublemakers. Monkeys.

MATTHEW: Feeling better?

NEGRO: A bit better. Whoever you are, thank you, thank you. But you must hide me; there's a lynching mob on my trail!

PUERTO RICAN: *aside*. Muy bien.

MATTHEW: I thought as much. But no lynching mob is going to cross my threshold.

PUERTO RICAN: *muttering*. Musta raped a white virgin.

METTHEW: Did you say something, Mr. García?

PUERTO RICAN: Nothing, amigo, I was belching.

MATTHEW: Nanny, don't forget our guest while I attend to Mr. — —

NEGRO: Nguyo Lubumbo. Ambassador of Zimbustan.

MATTHEW: Ambassador of Zimbustan! I don't know what to say. How did you — how did this — ?

NANNY: Here's a cup of coffee, Mr. Lubumbo. I'm honored. Welcome in my country's name.

PUERTO RICAN: *between his teeth*. Nigger.

NEGRO: Thank you, but really, you must conceal me somewhere, I implore you. I'm too weak to fight back. If they find me I'm done for.

MATTHEW: *to* NANNY. Take a quick look outside.

NANNY: *looking out.* Nothing yet. A bit of dust in the distance, that's all.

NEGRO: It must be them! Oh my God, if only I had strength enough to blow this whistle. *He has a whistle around his neck.* Nobody is going to help me.

MATTHEW: Of course we're going to help you. You're in the house of Matthew Available —

NEGRO: Delighted.

MATTHEW: — who will fight for the downtrodden till the last flake of his body turns to dust. But tell me, Mr. Lubumbo, why this vicious mob is hunting you.

NEGRO: I hardly know.

PUERTO RICAN: *under his breath.* I bet.

NEGRO: I was standing on a street corner with the Cultural Attaché of the Cameroon, reminiscing about our days at Trinity, when a pretty girl walked by in front of us.

PUERTO RICAN: *setting his lunch tray down and standing up.* White?

NEGRO: Yes. I laughed and said, "What a pretty girl." A policeman happened to overhear me. He yelled Rape! and suddenly it seemed as if the entire population was down on us, howling, shaking sticks, spitting, throwing stones.

NANNY: How did you get away?

NEGRO: Tom Boyo, my Cameroonian friend, had his open sports coupé parked at the curb. He jumped in and drove off. This diverted the mob long enough for me to run the other way. I ran, I ran, I ran, and now I'm almost dead, I can't even blow this whistle.

MATTHEW: Why the whistle?

NEGRO: To rally my people.

PUERTO RICAN: *aside to* MATTHEW. Are you gonna stand for this?

MATTHEW: No, Mr. García. We'll all defend him against that mob.

PUERTO RICAN: *roaring.* That ain't what I meant!

MATTHEW: What's the matter, Mr. García? You look mighty upset.

PUERTO RICAN: Sangre de Dios! He don't even knock to come in, he's steaming hot after raping a white virgin, he talks about whistling for his Africans —

MATTHEW: Gently, amigo, we're all equal, black, white, and, if I may say so, brown, like you.

PUERTO RICAN: Brown? Brown? Who's brown? I'm pure Spanish, I'm Andaluz, white, pure white, you're slandering me.

MATTHEW: All right, Mr. García, you're any color you choose. Nanny, go to the kitchen. I want you to fix a good solid lunch for Mr. Lubumbo.

NANNY: I hate to tell you, Mr. Matthew.

MATTHEW: What?

NANNY: All I've got left is a few steaks in the freezer, and it'll take two hours to thaw them out.

NEGRO: My dear, dear lady, I assure you I don't need a thing. Just hide me, or let me die in peace.

MATTHEW: Nonsense; there's going to be a fight, and we must fatten you up for it. There's enough left on Mr. García's tray for two lunches.

PUERTO RICAN: That's *my* tray!

MATTHEW and NANNY: Mr. García!

PUERTO RICAN: *My* tray!

MATTHEW: *trying to seize the tray.* If you don't mind.

PUERTO RICAN: *roaring.* No nigger is gonna eat offa my tray!

MATTHEW: May I point out —

PUERTO RICAN: Who they think they are? Go back to Africa! This country is for white men!

MATTHEW: And here I thought that you Latin Americans were free of these prejudices.

PUERTO RICAN: Sure, prejudices is for Yankees. We're not allowed to have 'em.

MATTHEW: You're getting offensive, Mr. García, now that I've fed you. Give me that tray.

PUERTO RICAN: Over my dead body. I don't like niggers and I don't like nigger-lovers! Wait! I'll call that mob myself! And let the blacks stay where they belong. Under *us*. D'you hear? Down on their knees, up in the trees, back to the plantations!

MATTHEW: Give me that tray and shut up.

PUERTO RICAN: Back to slavery!

NEGRO: *feebly*. We'll kill you all.

PUERTO RICAN: *flinging himself on the* NEGRO. Like hell you will! Hijo de puta!

NEGRO: Help! He's killing me!

MATTHEW: Nanny, help!

NANNY: Mr. García, you're a Christian!

PUERTO RICAN: Damn right I'm a Christian! That's why I'll murder the voodoo heathen!

NEGRO: Arghhh!

MATTHEW: *fighting the* PUERTO RICAN. Take your hands off my guest! *They exchange blows.* Nanny, he's bloodied my eye!

NANNY: Watch the gueridon!

PUERTO RICAN: Ouch!

MATTHEW: We'll see.

PUERTO RICAN: Ouch! White nigger!

MATTHEW: Nanny, hit him with the Justice Unbound!

NANNY: I will. *She does so and lays the* PUERTO RICAN *out flat.*

MATTHEW: *staggering to a chair.* Fighting for the oppressed is no holiday.

NEGRO: *feebly.* Jolly good work, Mr. Available. If only I could have helped.

MATTHEW: Don't mention it, Mr. Lubumbo. Nanny, give me that glass of wine.

NANNY: I'm bleeding too.

MATTHEW: *bathing his eye.* My robe is torn.

NEGRO: I can only apologize for the untimely intrusion.

MATHEW: Oh no, I assure you, I'm honored to have you in my house, Mr. Ambassador.

NEGRO: You are an honor to your country, to your race, and to mankind.

NANNY: What'll we do with Mr. García?

MATTHEW: The ruffian. Let's drag him out. Is he still breathing?

NANNY: I'm afraid so. *They pull him out.*

MATTHEW: Come on, Nanny, do your bit for a change, will you?

NANNY: Sorry, Mr. Matthew, my arm hurts. May I lock the door now?

MATTHEW: Never. Go on, feed our guest.

NANNY: I don't know that we should, Mr. Matthew.

MATTHEW: Why not?

NANNY: Do I have to remind you what happened when you fed the others?

MATTHEW: Isn't that just like you? Egotistical old maid. Nothing counts for you except your own hide. I don't know why I'm even answering you. Now, Mr. Lubumbo, can we induce you to take a little refreshment?

NEGRO: The mob, Mr. Available, the mob. Won't you try to hide me in a cellar or an attic?

MATTHEW: The mob has no earthly reason to stop at this particular house. But if they do, I'll beat them back, don't worry. Come now, take some food. You said yourself you needed strength to blow your whistle.

NEGRO: True.

MATTHEW: Of course, I'd gladly blow it for you.

NEGRO: Oh no! That's for me to do. I *will* have a bite after all. Very good of you. *He begins to eat.*

MATTHEW: Nanny, stop fiddling with your wound and prepare some fresh coffee.

NEGRO: Oh, splendid.

Exit NANNY.

MATTHEW: I recommend this Port Salut.

NEGRO: Excellent. I feel the vital spirits starting to course again in my veins.

MATTHEW: You are here on a mission, Mr. Lubumbo?

NEGRO: *Dr.* Lubumbo. Yes, I am. My country is seeking military aid — the usual hardware, I'm afraid — aircraft — tanks — one day, you know, we shall have to exterminate South Africa. A dreary business. Oh my, I'm still very weak. Quite dizzy and all that.

MATTHEW: Nanny, hurry the coffee!

NANNY: *from the kitchen.* Coming up!

MATTHEW: Another slice of ham will help, Dr. Lubumbo. You know, it's simply thrilling to think of all these proud new independent nations. Only a few years ago, you were smarting under the boot of the white colonials, and now here you are, Malawi, Cameroon, the Congo, Gabon, Zambia, Botswana, and so on. I love to roll the exotic names off my tongue.

NEGRO: You are a well-informed man, Mr. Available. *Nanny has come in with the coffee.* Thank you so much, my good woman. Two lumps, that's it. Smashing lunch. What was I saying? Oh yes, that you are a well-informed man.

MATTHEW: I try to be.

NEGRO: And well disposed toward us.

MATTHEW: Indeed I am.

NEGRO: Ours is a hard struggle.

MATTHEW: But a splendid one too. Already, I'm sure, free Zimbustan has doubled, tripled, quadrupled its resources.

NEGRO: Not quite, perhaps. But today, when a Zimbu starves, at least he starves at the hands of another Zimbu.

MATTHEW: Tremendous.

NANNY: I don't call that much of an improvement.

MATTHEW: Don't meddle in what's beyond you, Nanny. I think it's encouraging.

NEGRO: Most encouraging.

NANNY: What about that posse that's out looking for you, Mr. Lubumbo? Ain't you afraid of it anymore?

NEGRO: *fingering his whistle.* Dr. Lubumbo. No, I'm no longer afraid. *He has grown noticeably larger and stronger.*

MATTHEW: You do look remarkably improved, I'm happy to say.

NEGRO: Perhaps I'd better go. You've been most helpful, and I shan't forget it.

MATTHEW: Please don't mention it. Nanny, take a look outside again to make sure those maniacs have scattered.

NANNY: Sure. *She looks outside.* I guess you'd better hide Mr. Lubumbo in the wardrobe. There's a mob closing in on us. They're banging on doors and raising the devil.

MATTHEW: *grabbing the poker.* Here's the wardrobe, Dr. Lubumbo.

NEGRO: That won't be necessary anymore. I believe I can manage now.

Shouts outside.

A VOICE: If he's anywhere in town, that's where he's got to be, fellers. Egghead House.

VOICES: Let's go in and get him out. Lynch the nigger! Bash in the door!

NEGRO: Steady on, Mr. Available. Courage, madam. I shall manage.

NANNY: There's a sturdy oak tree in front of the house, Mr. Lubumbo; that's what scares me.

NEGRO: I'm glad you mentioned it, my dear; I intend to make good use of it.

VOICE: Easy there, don't jostle, one guy is all we need. Go on in, Officer Slotnik.

Violent entrance of a burly Policeman.

POLICEMAN: Where's that —? *He sees the Negro and shouts to the people outside.* Don't nobody need to follow me. I got him. I got him good. *Uproar outside. The Policeman whips out a couple of pistols.* Okay, mister, come out quiet, no use puttin up a fight. You got a date with a noose.

MATTHEW: *standing in front of the Negro.* Over my dead body.

POLICEMAN: I'll sure be glad to oblige.

NANNY: *screams.* No!

NEGRO: *moving Matthew aside.* Let me handle this. Here I am, officer. Remember I enjoy diplomatic immunity, but I'm ready to follow you.

VOICE: What's going on in there, Slotnik?

VOICE: Need any help?

POLICEMAN: Relax, boys, lemme handle this my own way. *To the Negro.* All right, black boy, get your black ass out through that door, and we'll converse about your diplomatic unity from the end of a rope.

MATTHEW: Officer, for God's sake! This is the Ambassador of Zimbustan!

POLICEMAN: If he's the Ambassador of Bustown, let him call his pals out.

NEGRO: *in the doorway.* That is precisely my intention. *He blows his whistle.*

POLICEMAN: Whadda ya think you're doin? Calling a fucking taxicab? Come and get him, fellers! Here he is! *He shoves the Negro out, leaves after him, slams the door. Uproar outside, shots.*

VOICE: Don't shoot the guy before we've strung him up!

VOICE: Smith, hold the rope!

VOICE: We got us a nigger!

VOICE: Yippee!

VOICE: No more white girls for the black bastard! *Other shouts ad libitum.*

MATTHEW: I'm sick. What can we do? Call the police! Oh God, that *was* the police! Nanny, I can't, look out the window, tell me what's going on.

NANNY: Oh Jesus Christ, oh Jesus Christ, save him, they've bound his wrists, they've torn off his necktie. Now what? Merciful God! What's this? What's this? Mr. Matthew, oh oh oh oh, come here, quick —

MATTHEW: I can't. . . .

NANNY: Come here I tell you! Dozens of blacks running to the rescue! Hundreds! Thousands! Millions! *Matthew rushes to the window.*

MATTHEW: Ha! The whistle! Nanny, the whistle did it! Hurrah!

NANNY: Don't go out, Mr. Matthew, please! *A new kind of uproar outside.*

VOICE: They're comin down from every side!

VOICE: Run for your lives!

VOICES: Shoot! Shoot! Don't wait!

VOICE: Hold it!

VOICE: Africans! Forward! Lynch 'em! Don't let the white bastards escape! Shoot into the groins! Shoot into the eyes! *Shots.*

VOICE: Help, help! Stop!

NANNY: They're stringing up the policeman!

POLICEMAN: *outside.* Men, they're lynchin' me. Call out the National Guard! Aaargh . . . *Shouts of triumph. More shots. Matthew's windows are shattered.*

VOICE: Destroy the white man!

LIVING ROOM WITH 6 OPPRESSIONS

NANNY: Behind the sofa, Mr. Matthew! Oh Jesus Christ, the world's coming to an end! *Enter Lubumbo. He smashes all the furniture.*

NEGRO: Nothing personal, you understand.

NANNY: The gueridon!

NEGRO: Personally, I'm most grateful to you both. *He knocks down a last vase and leaves.*

VOICE: How many are swinging, men?

VOICE: Fifteen!

VOICE: Down with white imperialism!

VOICE: Freedom!

VOICE: Power!

VOICE: Dignity!

VOICE: Fifteen in a row. Ain't they handsome!

VOICE: Here's another one!

VOICE: Don't let him get away! Fire!

NANNY: Don't move, Mr. Matthew!

VOICE OF VICTIM: Not me! *A shot, and then a white man's body is tossed into Matthew's house.*

NANNY: Oh Jesus Christ!

MATTHEW: I think they're finished, Nanny. *The roars have diminished.*

Presently all is silent. Matthew and Nanny come out of hiding and examine the body.

MATTHEW: Is he dead?

NANNY: Must be.

MATTHEW: Let's place him on the table. Maybe we can still help. Oh God, what a Sunday afternoon! *They lift the body to the table.*

MATTHEW: Careful with all those splinters.

NANNY: He won't mind, poor man. Oh, Mr. Matthew, there's a card in his vest pocket.

MATTHEW: Let me see it. "Innocent Bystander." What do you make of that?

NANNY: I think it's odd.

MATTHEW: I don't know. I'm beginning to feel, I don't know, as if I'd made a mistake somewhere.

The Innocent Bystander sits up.

INNOCENT BYSTANDER: I'm glad to hear you say that, Mr. Available. *He shakes hands with Matthew and Nanny.* How do you do. How do you do. I hope I haven't been too much bother.

MATTHEW: *dazed.* No-no . . . Lunch?

INNOCENT BYSTANDER: Most certainly not. I only dropped in, so to speak. But now I'd better be on my way. No need to see me out, thank you. Oh yes. After I'm gone, I suggest—. *He makes a gesture.*

NANNY: Lock the door?

INNOCENT BYSTANDER: Uhuh. *He lights a cigarette.*

MATTHEW: My door?

INNOCENT BYSTANDER: Your door.

MATTHEW: And then? What then?

INNOCENT BYSTANDER: Bang bang. Somebody knocks. Who's there? You take a look through the peephole. Another look. And then another look. And then maybe you open sometimes a little.

MATTHEW: And the lunches?

INNOCENT BYSTANDER: Small lunches. So long, my friends. *The handle comes off the door; he tosses it away.* Beautiful junk heap you've got here. Tut tut.

He leaves. There is a long pause. Matthew hesitates. He looks at Nanny, who is beginning to take in the shambles, then he goes to the door and locks it.

MATTHEW: We'll replace the doorknob and fix the windows. *Nanny picks up the gueridon and begins to cry.* It's a junk heap all right.

NANNY: *crying over the gueridon.* Your mother and me bought it together.

MATTHEW: There, there now.

NANNY: *sobbing.* And look at the commode, Mr. Matthew, your grandad's it was, lousy Victorian he always called it, every leg broken. Look at our clock. Look at the glass doors. Look at these chairs. Look, look, look. I can't believe it. All your things, Mr. Matthew, every day for thirty-five years I dusted everything.

Matthew is staring at Nanny.

MATTHEW: *in a small voice.* You're bleeding.

NANNY: *still crying.* I don't care. They even ripped the carpet.

MATTHEW: Sure you care, with all that dust and dirt.

NANNY: I've got a clean handkerchief.

MATTHEW: Give it to me. *He bandages her.* But you've got to stop crying.

NANNY: I'll try.

MATTHEW: We have to pick up the pieces, you and me.

NANNY: Thirty-five years of work wasted.

MATTHEW: Maybe not. Who can tell? You promised to stop crying, though.

NANNY: I'll stop, Mr. Matthew.

MATTHEW: How's this for a bandage?

NANNY: Fine.

MATTHEW: We should have used iodine.

NANNY: I don't care.

MATTHEW: Sit down a bit. You've had a rough day. Sit down.

NANNY: Me?

He stares at her.

NANNY: Anything the matter with you, Mr. Matthew?

MATTHEW: Why?

NANNY: You're looking at me as if you'd never seen me before.

MATTHEW: Nanny . . .

NANNY: Yes, Mr. Matthew?

MATTHEW: *in a very small voice.* What's your name?

NANNY: *dumbfounded, remembers.* Bertha. Bertha Robbins.

CURTAIN

Simultaneous Transmissions

ROBERT PATRICK

SIMULTANEOUS TRANSMISSIONS was seen at Kranny's Nook, 782 Union Street, Brooklyn, New York, in March, 1973. The production was directed by Marjorie Melnick and the company included Keith Fox, Merriman Gatch, Clyde Kelley, J. R. Marks, Ann Saxman, Susan Spector, Gayle Zelazny and Joseph Zwerling. Set and Lighting was by Brian Jayne, Assistant to the Director was Richard Kreston and the Prop Master was John Kelly. Sounds were by Helen Englehardt, Tom Giles and Lou Wainfeld.

Other production: Trinity Church, June, 1973, directed by Jean Forest.

SIMULTANEOUS TRANSMISSIONS is dedicated to M. G. Escher.

Approximate playing time: 10 minutes

No set required. At each side of the stage is a family, consisting of a MOTHER, *a* FATHER, *and a teenage* SON.

PARENTS: There they are. Look at them looking at us. Who knows what they're up to?

SONS: Who are they? Mother? Father? What do they want?

PARENTS: Who knows what they want? You know what they want? I know what they want.

SONS: Tell me. I want to know.

PARENTS: They want to take our things away from us.

SONS: Don't they have any things of their own?

PARENTS: Yes, they do! And no, they don't! They have plenty, but they want ours! They have nothing, but they want what we've got!

SONS: What have they got that's good?

PARENT: They have nothing that we want, and they wouldn't give it to us anyway. They have things we want and we can get it out of them! We don't want anything they've got, and besides, we need it! We don't want anything to do with them; how dare they prey into our lives? Besides, we want to be friends with them; how dare they be so stand-offish?

SONS: I don't understand. It does not compute. Tell me what you mean.

PARENTS: Of course you don't understand; you're younger. I'm older; I know what I mean.

THE SCENE

Brian Jayne's floor plan for **Simultaneous Transmissions**, performed at Kranny's Nook. Using platforms, Jayne and Director Marjorie Melnick transformed a long, narrow coffee shop into a theatre with three integrated playing areas. The platforms were scaled as follows: A = 5 feet; B = 45 inches; C = 36 inches; D = 27 inches; E = 18 inches; F = 9 inches.

SONS: I understand; you understand.

PARENTS: Then understand this: we've got to do something about them.

SONS: I don't understand; what is it you think they're doing?

PARENT: They're watching us; they're talking about us.

SONS: We're watching them; we're talking about them.

PARENTS: But they're watching us all the time. Watch them watch us. Look, try this simple test: We'll turn away, then when we turn back you'll see that they're watching us. Now, turn away.

SONS *turn away. The two sets of* PARENTS *wave to each other, smiling.*

PARENTS: Now turn around. See? They're watching us.

SONS: Wow! You're right. But — were they watching us all the time?

PARENTS: Yes, yes.

SONS: How do you know?

PARENT: Do you doubt us? We were watching them.

SONS: How could I ever doubt you? What shall we do?

PARENTS: You must go and fight them. I am needed here at home. I fear they plan an invasion.

SONS: If you say so.

PARENT: But your military training must be secret from them. Close your eyes and do what we say.

SONS: My eyes are closed; what shall I do?

The SONS *advance with their eyes closed and have a mock-battle in accord with the next speech. The* SONS *never quite touch each other during this pantomimed battle.*

PARENTS: He is directly before you. Stab him with your bayonet. Shove his filthy carcass off your weapon. Shoot him in the head. Stab him in the gut. Hold him down and pull your bayonet out. Kick him in the teeth. Hop on his head. Leave him on the battlefield, dead, dead, dead! Now, come home to us. Follow our voices home!

SONS: Can I open my eyes now?

PARENTS: Yes, yes, my boy, your training is complete. Now are you ready to go?

SONS: I guess so. Are they ready?

PARENTS: Yes. I have it on secret authority that they've been training, too. They're going to sneak up on us if we don't attack. It's up to you now.

SONS: I hope that I can do it.

PARENTS: Do it!

SONS: I hope that I can win!

PARENTS: Win!

SONS: It's all been games 'til now.

PARENTS: Now!

SONS: Now the real tests begin!

PARENTS: Begin!

During the next speeches the SONS *move toward and past each other, and perform the described actions on the opposite* PARENTS, *who are taken by surprise and killed.*

PARENTS: Advance with your weapon. There is the enemy. Protect me from him. He is directly before you. Stab him with your bayonet!

SONS: Shove his filthy carcass off my weapon. Shoot him in the head. Stab him in the gut. Hold him down and pull my bayonet out. Kick him in the teeth. Hop on his head. Leave him on the battlefield, dead, dead, dead! *The* SONS *wander aimlessly around the stage.* Daddy? Mommy? Can I open my eyes now?

CURTAIN

OOB TRENDS

Surveying directors and producers on current Off-Off Broadway trends, *The Scene* found

- Preoccupation with the great American violence
- Whelming of black theatre
- Movement to synthesize the physical theatre with literary theatre
- Movement away from sex/nudity

VIOLENCE/ The prevalence of dramatic violence provokes mixed reactions among directors and producers, but consensus is that, like it or not, it will rage undiminished on our scene. Indeed many, seeing it as ingrained in the American character, are convinced of the necessity for exploring it, finding new artistic perspective for it. As Richard Schechner of The Performance Group observed, "Violence has always been a part of the American experience as introduced into this continent by the rapacious European settlers and their slaves who were themselves stolen through war and rape from Africa. The problem is not to end violence but to make it less harmful."

Violence, furthermore, was seen, not only in terms of historical and contemporary effects, but as a principle to be accommodated in creation. Ken Eulo, artistic director of Courtyard Playhouse, stated esthetic aims in terms of violence: "Theatre isn't violent enough. When two moving objects clash, there is usually a reaction. The bigger the object, the more violent the reaction. What the theatre (Off-Off Broadway as well as all other theatre) needs is bigger vision, creating bigger characters—thereby creating a more violent reaction."

While the phenomenon of exploitive or gratuitous violence was often deplored, the dramatic validity of the preoccupation was admitted.

OOB TRENDS

Wilford Leach, artistic director of La Mama, summed up this situation: "Gratuitous violence, like gratuitous sex and nudity, isn't particularly interesting, since we've had a surfeit of it for itself. On the other hand, all three are, inevitably, fascinating onstage and off."

But spokesmen for two black theatres deplored the tendency. Ernie McClintock of Afro-American Studio Theatre Centre said simply, "Let's do away with violence." Robert Macbeth of New Lafayette Theatre commented: "There will be violence in the arts as long as there is violence in the world/theatre. Violence ends in destruction on both levels."

BLACK THEATRE/ The emergence of the black experience as a potent force in drama is the simple fact announced by playwright-director Ed Bullins of Black Theatre Workshop when asked to cite the trends "just now surfacing." The number of black theatres has impressively increased, their influence widening. As avant garde critic Donald Phelps predicted in 1969, the greatest artistic achievements of the blacks during the 70's might be in drama: "close to the momentum of actuality, with a sense of physical commitment." Background: While emphatically positive about his own efforts at New Lafayette, Robert Macbeth sees OOB as a whole merely "an industrial complex which provides materials and people for the larger industrial complex of Broadway and the final giant movies/Hollywood." He believes the art of theatre and the industry that uses it are both dying and will "soon be buried under the garbage of world confusion and stupidity."

PHYSICAL THEATRE? *The Scene s*aw a general disenchantment with physical theatre per se, and movement toward synthesis with literary theatre. While the question on violence typically elicited the most passionate and eloquent responses, the question on physical theatre produced the most elaborate answers. One exception was characteristically cryptic Ed Bullins who said, "The writer will dominate soon."

Edward Berkeley of Shade Company remarked: "The question is based on a fallacy. OOB has not created anything near a 'style,' just some ill-rehearsed gymnastics—hardly a whole style." He sees a trend toward "more bad theatres destroying some good actors and encouraging many bad actors (and directors, playwrights and designers)."

Richard Schechner defined the synthesis: "I hope the physical theatre will be seen as compatible with the literary theatre; that properly handled they are each dimensions of the other." He sees a trend "towards a more popular theatre, towards concentarting on performing itself as a style (presentation, vaudeville, circus, story-telling)." Yet the phenomenon of physical theatre is very much with us for now. Ken Eulo said, "People have been masturbating for two thousand years. I don't see why it should stop now. Language doesn't seem to satisfy the norm."

Wilford Leach of La Mama, a theatre long virtually synonomous with avant garde, argued a position that many of his colleagues now regard as rear guard: "The term 'playwright' has been enlarged considerably beyond that rather narrow modern one which meant the person who wrote the text and stage directions. There are more and more 'wrights' who are more like the director in the motion picture—that is, who may or may not write dialogue, but who are the primary creator and conceptual talent. These 'wrights' are as truly playwrights as anyone who ever wrote a play.

"The ideas of physical theatre were an interesting antidote to the conventions of the plays and production modes of the past thirty years or so, but it is now very familiar and no longer holds much interest *in itself*. I doubt that the theatre will become more literary if you mean more like the usual run of plays of the 20's and 40's and 50's, but if on the other hand you mean have something in common with Shakespeare or Moliere or Brecht or Sheridan or any of the more remarkable playwrights of the past, I would say definitely yes. But the point is, it isn't possible to *do* the same thing by *imitating* them."

Leach contended that "in general the term 'trends' is an unfortunate one, since it puts value on fashion. Quality can't be equated with newness. Better concentrate on the values and aspirations of new work. It is at this point that the finest work of the past and present—and probably future—are really very similar."

SEX/NUDITY: The most frequent response to the theatrical flesh market contained the word "boring." Now that OOB has gone all-the-way, now that the main freedom-of-expression issues seem at least temporarily settled, considerable negative reaction or unresponsiveness is usual among the directors. Ken Eulo says, "The human body is like a subway train—you've seen one, you've seen them all." He asks, "How long can people watch the same thing?"

Wilford Leach commented, "Sex/nudity in itself doesn't any longer attract attention. There *may* be more of it, but not for the same reasons."

Most agree, however, that it's on the way out in its sensational aspects. Edward Berkeley noted, "It is now an accepted part of all plays." He is one of the minority, though, who saw it "slowly growing *more* evident."

Richard Schechner was one who agreed that the trend toward sex/nudity has reached its peak—"for the time being." He said, "It was a breakthrough when it happened. It has now been co-opted by the porn films. There will probably be a period of extreme censorship and then a new step toward full expressivity in theatre. Whenever something is used as a hype or as a means of exploitation—for money, for success, for notoriety—it needs to be reassessed, but not thrown away."

THE CONTRIBUTION OF OOB: Predictably much was said about OOB's functions in terms of the presentation of new playwrights, providing a fertile realm of alternatives to Broadway and its limited produce, serving as a training ground with experimental stations, to entertain audiences at low prices, etc. As Ed Bullins said, "Off-Off Broadway serves so many functions that one or several functions are less than reality."

Wilford Leach contributed this candid look at the scene: "Since Off-Off Broadway productions are done on very modest budgets—as compared to the commercial stage—there is, relatively speaking, little commercial pressure and considerable artistic freedom. Though no one working on OOB *need* conform, it's fair to say that there's considerable social pressure to be part of the latest new thing, that the *Voice* critics are taken very seriously, that almost everyone is trying to get a grant of some kind from *some* institution, that there's a degree of the buddy system, and that a low budget *does* restrict what can be done. In other words, there are definitely strong pressures, and people working OOB conform to them to a greater or lesser degree. Similarly, while OOB offers greater artistic freedom, it offers equally the opportunity for greater self-indulgence. The chief virtue of Off-Off Broadway is that anyone who can find a space in which to perform can declare himself part of Off Off Broadway. It can be wonderful or unbearable, fresh or exciting or indulgent and talentless. It's a spring garden in which both flowers and weeds grow abundantly. At least it has the possibility of being, except for the budgetary limitations, as good as the talent and taste and integrity of the people who work in it, and the commercial stage seldom allows that."

One Act, Five Scenes

Because of the sheer abundance of new plays produced Off-Off Broadway each year, it's virtually impossible to publish a collection of this kind without a nagging feeling that several worthy scripts have not been chosen. It's equally frustrating to encounter a deserving longer work that can't be included because of space limitations.

While there is no way of solving the first problem without attending almost every OOB production of an original play, we felt there was at least a halfway solution to the problem of longer works. That would be to publish a representative portion of the play. Admittedly, some of the larger impact is lost with this approach, but at least the particular felicity of style can be savored and the microcosm can give a fairly true picture of the total work.

The following section contains the entire first act of Joseph Renard's "The Wrath Of God," as well as representative scenes from "The New York Transit Authority" by Joseph Lazarus, "The Women's Representative" by Sun Yu, "Applejuice" by Francine Trevens, "Mrs. Peacock" by Stanley Nelson and "The Blasphemy of Rimbaud's Sister" by Robert Herron and Alexander Gotfryd. All but the latter are full-length plays; "Blasphemy" is a long one-acter. We've tried to select segments that are reasonably cohesive and self-contained in themselves.

It's interesting that three of these plays were presented at houses—The Joseph Jefferson Theatre, The Night House, Theatre 77 Rep—that were just in their infancy when *The Scene/1* was published, while the other three houses—WPA, Bastiano's, New York Theatre Ensemble—have weathered the vicissitudes of OOB for some years now. We like this meld of the old and the new, finding in it still another indication of the continuing vitality of Off-Off Broadway.

THE EDITORS

The Wrath of God

JOSEPH RENARD

THE WRATH OF GOD was seen at WPA, 333 Bowery, New York City, in November, 1973. The production was directed by Hugh Gittens and featured the following actors:

BILDAD/DISCIPLE	Craig Barish
MRS. JOB/ENSEMBLE	Nicki Berke
ADAM/DISCIPLE	Ron Carrier
ROMAN SOLDIER	John Clarkson
GOD	Jim Doerr
SATAN/JUDAS/SERPENT	John Fallon
ELIPHAZ/DISCIPLINE	Hank Flacks
THE VIRGIN MARY	Loretta Fraioli
EVE/ENSEMBLE	Elena Hall
ZOPHAR/DISCIPLE	Stephen E. M. Early
SERVANT/DISCIPLE	Redvers Jeanmarie
SERVANT/DISCIPLE	David Kalish
JOHN THE DISCIPLE	Joaquin LaHabana
JOB/DISCIPLE	Nicholas Levitin
JESUS	Gary Swartz
MARY MAGDALENE	Dorothy Somekh
SERVANT/DISCIPLE	Wyn Warren
ROMAN SOLDIER	Walter Wood

AUTHOR'S ACKNOWLEDGEMENT: Although his interpretation of the Judeo-Christion myth may not be what its progenitors had in mind, Mr. Renard nevertheless wishes to acknowledge his deep and compounding indebtedness to God the Almighty; to the cosmically attuned authors of the Book of Genesis and the Book of Job; to the saintly storytellers Matthew, Mark, Luke and John; and last and forever to the translators who under King James delivered the Holy Bible into majestic, unsurpassable English.

THE WRATH OF GOD

ACT I

Total darkness.

VOICE OF GOD: What do you want to do tonight, Satan?

VOICE OF SATAN: I don't know, God, what do you want to do?

VOICE OF GOD: I don't know, Satan, what do you want to do?

VOICE OF SATAN: I don't know, God, what . . . what in Your name are we going on like this for?

VOICE OF GOD: What else is there to do?

VOICE OF SATAN: Oh, I don't know. Pass me the nectar. *Sound of pouring, drinking.* We could go to your harem in heaven and pluck some angel feathers.

VOICE OF GOD: My harem? Are you kidding? Those fat, sexless neuters? I've been looking at them forever. I haven't seen a new face in seventy-seven billion centuries. I'm bored. I'm telling you, I'm bored with it all. Nothing to eat but manna. Manna in the morning, manna in the evening, manna at suppertime. It's driving me insane! If only I could kill myself. But I'm as indestructible as I'm omnipotent.

VOICE OF SATAN: We could dream up some new tortures for the damned.

VOICE OF GOD: What's the use? We've put those poor little devils through hell for so long there's no more fun in it. Their nerves have been shot for aeons. In fact, I think most of them have become masochists. There's nothing that most of them would like better than to have a pitchfork stuck up their ass and be dropped into a vat of boiling shit.

VOICE OF SATAN: I know how we can get an endless supply of hypersensitive innocents to torture.

VOICE OF GOD: How?

VOICE OF SATAN: You could create the world.

VOICE OF GOD: The world? What's that?

VOICE OF SATAN: Well how should I know?—until you've created it.

VOICE OF GOD: How do you create the world?

VOICE OF SATAN: I thought you were omniscient. I thought you knew everything.

VOICE OF GOD: You can be omniscient and still have a bad memory.

VOICE OF SATAN: God, you know something? You're dumb. Dumb.

VOICE OF GOD: Why don't you create the world yourself if you know the magic formula, Prince?

VOICE OF SATAN: You know I don't have that power.

VOICE OF GOD: If you're so smart, why ain't you omnipotent?

VOICE OF SATAN: I'm perfectly happy being omniscient.

VOICE OF GOD: You know nothing about what it is to be God. The responsibility, the sleepless eternities, the . . .

VOICE OF SATAN: Do you want to go on complaining about your lot, or do you want to create the world?

VOICE OF GOD: All right, all right already. So tell me the magic formula.

VOICE OF SATAN: All right, God. Here we go. Repeat after me. "Let there be light."

VOICE OF GOD: Let there be light!

All the lights go up full, blindingly. Everything should be white. There should be a lower playing area for the humans, and a high heaven where God and Satan perch, with easy access from Heaven to Earth for Satan when he makes his periodic descents.

GOD: Hey, that's pretty good.

SATAN: Let there be a firmament in the midst of the waters,

GOD: Let there be a firmament in the midst of the waters,

SATAN: And let it divide the waters from the waters.

GOD: And let it divide the waters from the waters.

SATAN: Very good, God.

GOD: Oh, I'm in heaven. Let's call the firmament heaven.

SATAN: Let the waters under the heaven be gathered together unto one place,

GOD: Let the waters under the heaven be gathered together unto one place,

SATAN: And let the dry land appear.

GOD: And let the dry land appear.

SATAN: There it is.

GOD: Earthy, earthy. Let's call it earth.

SATAN: What about the water?

GOD: Let's call it . . . *sneezes* . . . seas. Good.

SATAN: Let the earth bring forth grass

GOD: Let the earth bring forth grass

SATAN: The herb yielding seed

GOD: The herb yielding seed

SATAN: And the fruit tree yielding fruit after his kind, whose seed is in itself.

GOD: And the fruit tree yielding fruit after his kind, whose seed is in itself.

SATAN: Let there be lights in the firmament of the heaven to divide the day from the night.

GOD: Let there be lights in the firmament of the heaven to divide the day from the night.

SATAN: And let them be for signs, and for seasons, and for days, and years.

GOD: And let them be for signs, and for seasons, and for days, and years.

SATAN: And let them be for lights in the firmament of the heaven to give light upon the earth.

GOD: And let them be for lights in the firmament of the heaven to give light upon the earth.

THE WRATH OF GOD

SATAN: Let the waters bring forth abundantly the moving creature that hath life,

GOD: Let the waters bring forth abundantly the moving creature that hath life,

SATAN: And fowl that may fly above the earth in the open firmament of heaven.

GOD: And fowl that may fly above the earth in the open firmament of heaven. Chicken every sunday. But you'll never get to heaven on a chicken.

SATAN: Let the earth bring forth the living creature after his kind:

GOD: Let the earth bring forth the living creature after his kind:

SATAN: Cattle, and creeping thing, and beast of the earth after his kind.

GOD: Cattle, and creeping thing, and beast of the earth after his kind.

SATAN: Let us make man in our image, after our likeness.

GOD: Let us make man in *my* image, after *my* likeness.

ADAM *appears.*

SATAN: And let him have dominion over the fish of the sea, and over the fowl of the air, and over the cattle,

GOD: And let him have dominion over the fish of the sea, and over the fowl of the air, and over the cattle,

SATAN: And over all the earth, and every thing that creepeth upon the earth after his kind.

GOD: And over all the earth, and over every creeping thing that creepeth upon the earth.

SATAN: You've done it.

GOD: I certainly have.

SATAN: Something's missing. I can't quite put my finger on it.

GOD: I've got it! He needs a helpmeet. It's no good that he should be alone. Why don't I create a woman for him?

SATAN: Why not?

GOD: Let there be woman. EVE *appears*. Be fruitful, and multiply, and replenish the earth, and subdue it: and have dominion over the fish of the sea, and over the fowl of the air, and over every living thing that moveth upon the earth. Behold, I have given you every herb bearing seed, which is upon the face of all the earth, and every tree, in the which is the fruit of a tree yielding seed; to you it shall be for meat. And to every beast of the earth, and to every fowl of the air, and to everything that creepeth upon the earth, wherein there is life. I have given every green herb for meat. And one final word, Adam and Eve. Never disobey my orders. Eternal life is yours, eternal bliss is yours, if you obey me. Otherwise, my wrath will cut you to ribbons. For now, I command you to do as you please, do whatever you want, and I command you to love life. The earth is yours. And yours is the gift of speech. I command you to name every living creature and every inanimate object, and every thought you have. The gift of speech. This alone is your priceless treasure. Use it. HE *withdraws to his throne.*

ADAM: Sky.

EVE: Cloud.

ADAM: Oak tree.

EVE: Bluebird.

ADAM: Sparrow.

EVE: Hummingbird.

ADAM: Robin.

EVE: Peach tree.

ADAM: Acorn.

EVE: Squirrel.

ADAM: Fox.

EVE: Daisy.

ADAM: Sunflower.

EVE: Lily.

ADAM: Rose.

EVE: Tulip.

ADAM: Chrysanthemum.

EVE: Hollyhock.

ADAM: Lilac.

EVE: Huckleberry.

ADAM: Strawberry.

EVE: Blackberry.

ADAM: Raspberry

EVE: Mulberry.

ADAM: Currant.

EVE: Cherry.

ADAM: Plum.

EVE: Pear.

ADAM: Lime.

EVE: Grapefruit.

ADAM: Kumquat.

EVE: Catnip.

ADAM: Cat.

EVE: Eeek! Mouse!

ADAM: Dog. Woof-woof!

EVE: Weeping willow.

ADAM: Magnolia.

EVE: Rhododendron.

ADAM: Carnation.

EVE: Hazlenut.

ADAM: Walnut.

EVE: Peanut.

ADAM: Juniper.

EVE: Honeysuckle.

ADAM: Dandelion.

EVE: Morning Glory.

ADAM: Jack-in-the-Pulpit.

EVE: Ivy.

ADAM: Sumac.

EVE: Wintergreen.

ADAM: Evergreen.

EVE: Spruce.

ADAM: Orange.

EVE: Apple.

ADAM: Eve.

EVE: Adam.

ADAM & EVE: Love. *They make love.*

GOD: Aren't they beautiful? Aren't they beautiful, Satan? They make me feel four hundred billion years younger. I feel like a young God again.

SATAN: Pass me the nectar. *He drinks.*

GOD: Aren't they beautiful? So young, and innocent, and worshipping of me? So incorruptible and obedient. Satan, you're a genius. I've got a whole new world to kick around.

SATAN: You say they're so incorruptible? So innocent?

GOD: It's true. They know nothing of the evil that you and I know. And I'll never torture them the way I do the damned. And they have genitals and copulation and love like no angel ever dreamed of. No knowledge of any difference between good and evil.

SATAN: Let's teach it to them.

GOD: No, I don't want to. They're innocent and incorruptible. And they obey me.

SATAN: Sure, they obey you. What did you tell them? Do whatever you please. Throw a few obstacles in their way and you're going to find a couple of sinners who find out what evil is when they feel the force of your righteous wrath.

GOD: Sheer balderdash.

SATAN: How do you know?

GOD: I trust them. I have faith in them.

SATAN: It's for them to have faith in you, not for you to have faith in them. I'll bet you anything that if you put them to the test, they'd fail it with fading colors.

GOD: What test?

SATAN: Any test. Anything. You've created what future generations will call a Frankenstein's monster there, Dr. God. I'm omniscient,

THE WRATH OF GOD

and I've already psyched out human nature. Forbid them to do something, anything, and they'll do it immediately, compulsively, blindly, as though their lives depended on it.

GOD: That's absurd, Satan. They're pure and innocent. They wouldn't dare do anything that I forbade them. I don't want to put them to any test.

SATAN: Put them to the test, I say. And put your money where your mouth is. I'll bet you 200 devils against 200 of your so-called angels that they'll fail the test.

GOD: You're on. What'll I test them with?

SATAN: Anything. It doesn't matter. The object doesn't matter. You could tell them not to eat an apple.

GOD: Done. The apple it is. I'll tell them it's the forbidden fruit, the fruit of the tree of the knowledge of good and evil.

SATAN: And I guarantee you, God, if they eat that apple they'll find out like lightning what evil is from you.

GOD: They'll never bite.

SATAN: I'll persuade them.

GOD: Persuade? Persuade? Who said anything about persuade. You just said they'd eat it if I forbade them. You're introducing a whole new series of rules here. The bet's off.

SATAN: No, no, don't pop through infinity. I gotta persuade them. We'll switch the odds. I'll give you five to two. Five hundred devils against 200 angels. Is that fair? Or do I have to get down on my knees and pray?

GOD: All right. Those two beauties can withstand anything. You jumped the gun. I'd have given you even money if you held out.

SATAN: It doesn't matter, because I'm going to win the bet anyway. Shall we begin?

GOD: Yes. Adam! Eve! *The lights come up on their sleeping bodies and they wake, rise, stretch, yawn, utterly satiated.*

ADAM & EVE: Yes, God.

GOD: I commanded you before to do as you please, to indulge yourselves thoroughly. Have you complied to the fullest?

ADAM & EVE: *Looking at each other adoringly.* Yes, God.

GOD: All right now. There's only one thing that I forbid you to do. Only one thing in the whole wide world that I forbid you to do.

ADAM & EVE: What's that, God?

GOD: You see that apple tree over there?

ADAM & EVE: Uh huh.

GOD: Don't you dare touch one of them apples. They're my private, special domain and I don't even call it an apple tree. I call it the tree of the knowledge of good and evil, which only me, me, me, do you understand—I'm the only one who gets to eat them apples. So don't you lay your grubby little hands on them, and don't you dare eat one of them, or I'll teach you a lesson that you'll never forget. I forbid you to eat the apple. Do you understand?

ADAM & EVE: Yes, God.

GOD: All right. Go your merry way, and we won't discuss this any further.

ADAM: *Approaching tree.* The Garden of Eden is so beautiful, Eve. I wonder why God values this apple tree over everything else around. The roses, for instance.

EVE: There must be something special about them. Apples must be the best thing in the whole garden, or God wouldn't want them all for himself.

ADAM: They are beautiful, you've got to admit. So plump, and red. I bet they're delicious. I wonder what would happen if we took one.

EVE: Don't even think about it, Adam. You know what God said. It's forbidden.

ADAM: I know, I know. But still. I'd like to find out what one tastes like. Maybe we could do it on the sly.

EVE: Don't be silly, Adam. God sees everything. We could never get away with it. Let's go pick some wild strawberries.

ADAM: I'm sick of them. I'm sick of everything except you and those weird apples. I'm going for a walk.

Exits. SATAN *enters, wrapped in a serpent skin. Eating an apple.*

SATAN: Delicious. Care for a bite?

EVE: No, thank you.

SATAN: Why not? It's a delicious apple. Please, please have a bite.

EVE: No, no, I can't.

THE WRATH OF GOD

SATAN: Why not.

EVE: It's because . . . who are you?

SATAN: I'm an old timer.

EVE: Life only started for me. Today. Forgive me if I don't know who you are.

SATAN: They call me Snakeeyes.

EVE: My name is Eve.

SATAN: Have some apple, Eve.

EVE: No, I really can't, you see, because God told us—me and Adam—that we mustn't eat any of those apples. They're his, he said, his alone, and I would no more touch one of those apples than I'd kill a butterfly.

SATAN: But this one is mine. I plucked it. I'm eating it. You don't see God objecting to that, do you? I'm one of his best friends. He lets me eat his apples. And if I offer a bite to you, where's the harm?

Offers apple.

EVE: It looks awfully good.

SATAN: Go ahead. Try it, you'll like it.

She bites into the apple.

EVE: It's delicious. Adam! Adam. *He enters.*

ADAM: Eve. What is it? Who's he?

EVE: Snakeyes.

SATAN: How do you do.

EVE: This is Adam. We are. We are.

ADAM: Lovers.

EVE: Friends.

ADAM: Husband and wife.

EVE: Bosom buddies.

SATAN: Have a taste, Adam. *proffering the apple.*

ADAM: No, no, no. We're not supposed to touch that. God said we can't have any.

SATAN: Who's God to tell you what to do? Aren't you your own boss? Anyway, your wife already had a bite. You see any change in her?

ADAM: You did?

EVE: It seemed . . . he said it was his apple, not God's. It's good, Adam. Nothing has happened to me. It's delicious. If anything happens, we might as well go down together, unless you want to leave me alone.

ADAM: I would never do that.

EVE: Have some. Try it. It's really a delicious apple.

SATAN *proffers the apple,* ADAM *eats.*

SATAN: God! You owe me 200 angels!

GOD: You filthy, obnoxious betrayers of your creator. You disobe-

THE WRATH OF GOD

dient, lying, hypocritical scum of the earth. You little worms, maggots who prey on the flesh of the living lord, your own creator. For this, you're going to suffer. Oh, am I going to make you suffer. You thought you had it made here, didn't you? Lounging around in the Garden of Eden all day with nothing to do but fuck and eat and sleep and admire the scenery. Well let me tell you, baby boy and girl, you've had it. You have had it. You dare to disobey me! You dare to eat my apple.

EVE: But he said. . . .

GOD: I don't give a fuck what Satan said. He was in on it.

ADAM: In on it? What do you mean.

GOD: None of your business, worm. Serpent. Sleazy, creepy, crawly thing. I want you to get the fuck out of my garden right now. I curse the day that I created you. You disobeyed me. You didn't follow my orders. What kind of perverts are you?

EVE: We only . . .

GOD: Shut up. And put on some clothes. It's indecent, the way you parade around with nothing one. Don't you have a sense of shame? *They arrange fig leaves.* You're ugly, do you understand? And you ought to be ashamed of yourselves.

ADAM: God, please, we didn't. . . .

GOD: You shut up, too. Oh, what a blow this is to me. I had such high hopes for you, Adam. And Eve. And Eve, I will greatly multiply thy sorrow and thy conception; in sorrow thou shalt bring forth children; and thy desire shall be to thy husband and he shall rule over thee.

ADAM: Well that's all right, God, but . . .

GOD: And because thou hast hearkened unto the voice of thy wife, and hast eaten of the tree, of which I commanded thee, saying Thou shalt not eat of it: cursed is the ground for thy sake; in sorrow shalt thou eat of it all the days of thy life; Thorns also and thistles shall it bring forth to thee; and thou shalt eat the herb of the field; In the sweat of thy face shalt thou eat bread, till thou return unto the ground; for out of it wast thou taken; for dust thou art and unto dust shalt thou return.

ADAM: Please, God, we meant no harm in eating your apple.

GOD: You dare to speak still. All right, I'll give you both barrels now. I told you both you were going to live forever, just like me. Well I've got a little bit of bad news for you. You're both gonna drop dead. That's right. I'm gonna kill you both. Not now. I'm going to let you worry about it. All the time. But you're going to have to drop dead. Death, do you understand? That's what you get for eating my apple! And all your children I'm going to kill too. And all your children's children—I'll kill them too, whenever I feel like it, with pestilence, murder, war, famine, cancer or whatever new disease I dream up. But you've had it. Go, go, go! Get out! Go East of Eden, to the land of nod, and scratch the barren soil for bean.

EVE: We're sorry, God.

GOD: Go!

ADAM: Will you have mercy on us?

GOD: Get out! Go drop dead!

They exit.

SATAN: That's two hundred angels you owe me.

GOD: How could they do this to me?

CURTAIN

The Blasphemy of Arthur Rimbaud's Sister

ROBERT HERRON AND ALEXANDER GOTFRYD

THE BLASPHEMY OF ARTHUR RIMBAUD'S SISTER was seen at the New York Theatre Ensemble, 2 East 2nd Street, New York City, in May, 1972. The production was directed by William Kushner and featured the following actors:

ARTHUR RIMBAUD	Jerry Zafer
ISABELLE	Stacy Scott
BRETAGNE	Paul Rosson
DJAMI	Norman Gibbs
SISTER DESJARDINS	Daphne Dyer
FATHER LEDOUX	Adrian Jack

Synopsis: ARTHUR RIMBAUD, *having foresaken poetry at age nineteen to become an engineer and businessman in Africa, has contracted gangrene in his leg and has returned to France. Now in his late twenties,* RIMBAUD *is dying in a Marseilles hospital room where he is attended by his sister,* ISABELLE, *and a hospital nurse,* SISTER DESJARDINS. BRETAGNE, *his childhood tutor, has been granted a private audience;* RIMBAUD *has stated that he is grateful for* BRETAGNE'S *tutelage during his early years.*

BRETAGNE: Ah! Grateful! *happy.* The *word* I came from Charleville hoping, desperately hoping to hear!

ARTHUR: *bemused.* That I'm grateful?

BRETAGNE: Ah, but yes.

ARTHUR: Then I am, I am.

BRETAGNE: Oh, prove it to me, Arthur. Prove your gratitude for our friendship through all these years, if friends we still remain.

ARTHUR: *at a total loss*. But I've said I'm grateful. What else can I do?

BRETAGNE: A small thing, Arthur, a minor, petty thing.

ARTHUR: Very well.

BRETAGNE: Name me your literary executor!

ARTHUR: *taken aback by the absurdity of the proposal*. My executor?

BRETAGNE: Someone must look after your reputation. You don't seem inclined to.

ARTHUR: Then, yes. By all means, Bretagne. Be thou my literary executor. What is it to me?

BRETAGNE: Ah, Arthur, how can I thank you enough.

ARTHUR: A trip from Charleville for this? You could have written a letter.

BRETAGNE: *businesslike*. Now, Arthur. If I am to manage your affairs, I must have the entire body of your work.

ARTHUR: *willing enough to cooperate*. I can't think clearly now. It was so long ago. Most of the poems were scattered about in journals and reviews. Mother might have kept copies of them. Or perhaps even Verlaine.

BRETAGNE: I have a bibliography of your published poems. And a good copy of *Season*.

ARTHUR: Then you've no problem.

BRETAGNE: *mischievously, he hopes.* None but you. Your unpublished poems, boy!

ARTHUR: There aren't any.

BRETAGNE: Come, come.

ARTHUR: I have not written a poem since I was nineteen.

BRETAGNE: *wagging his finger.* Don't try to fool an old friend. I don't believe you for a moment.

ARTHUR: Doubt if you wish, but there are no more poems.

BRETAGNE: Those trips to the Orient. Your years in Africa. Not a sensation in all that time? Never an urge to put an image on paper?

ARTHUR: I am a businessman. My writing was all on commercial orders.

BRETAGNE: Arthur, trust me. I am trying to confer upon you the immortality your genius deserves.

ARTHUR: My name will die like everybody else's.

BRETAGNE: But it mustn't. I won't allow it.

ARTHUR: None of it matters to me.

BRETAGNE: It *does* to some of us, Arthur — a great deal. You simply must understand. Why should I ask to be your executor if it were not important? Ah, Arthur. Trust me. Verlaine has made something of your name. And I shall magnify it to glory! I've already given it thought. The very first possible moment we must publish all your work in a single edition. Perhaps we'll play with doing *Season in Hell* by itself. *The Collected Poems and Prose Works of Arthur Rimbaud,* edited by Aristide Bretagne. It has a thunder to it, don't you think? Ah! They'll *all* sit up and take notice — not just Verlaine. And, so far as that goes, we'll put Verlaine in *his place.* You'd like that wouldn't you! Ho, ho, you can count on it: Verlaine is planning this very moment to edit your work himself. But we'll not let him get away with it. Thinks he can use *your* name to boost his own stock, does he? You know the popularity of his own poems is nothing to what it used to be. Ah, but he'll stand on your shoulders, quick enough. Reflected glory — that's all the man is after. But we'll confound him with our edition — the definitive, comprehensive Rimbaud.

ARTHUR: Let's not talk about it now, Bretagne. My leg has started again.

BRETAGNE: *heedless.* I've known you so long — and so well. Verlaine knew only your young passion. I know your soul! I gave it shape, molded it, kneaded it, stretched it, filled it — inspired it! *I* know the soul of Arthur Rimbaud. Who could edit your work better than I? But I must have it all, Arthur. Your genius is too great to stop itself. Give me your later poems, Arthur.

ARTHUR: There aren't any.

BRETAGNE: I know why you're being coy. Heh, afraid they're not up to the rest, are you? Genius fluctuates! We'll go over them together. If you're weary of them, perhaps I can — mend them myself. Oh, I know your style. They'll still be yours! But you must let me see them.

ARTHUR: *becoming fearful of Bretagne's intensity.* No . . .

BRETAGNE: You owe it to yourself, Arthur. You owe it to posterity. You owe it — yes, to me. In the name of our old friendship, give them to me. Arthur, I implore you. Do not deny an old friend this small favor. Where are they, Arthur? At Charleville, with your mother?

ARTHUR: No . . .

BRETAGNE: Or with that black devil what's-his-name in Africa? That *must* be where they are. Are they in Africa, Arthur? Tell me where they are. *Highly agitated.* Where are the poems!

ARTHUR: You're spitting in my face.

BRETAGNE: *grabs* ARTHUR: You owe them to me! You owe me the chance!

ARTHUR: *screaming.* Isabelle! Isabelle! Help me, Isabelle!

BRETAGNE: Help *me,* Arthur!

ARTHUR: Isabelle! Sister Desjardins! BRETAGNE *is blubbering on* ARTHUR'S *bed when Isabelle and Sister Desjardins rush in.*

ISABELLE: M. Bretagne!

DESJARDINS: Ah, M. Rimbaud. *Together they struggle to get* BRETAGNE *off the bed and out of the room.*

BRETAGNE: I'll give you immortality. In the name of God, Arthur . . .

ISABELLE: Mr. Bretagne, what have you done to my brother!

ARTHUR: Take him out. Take him away.

ISABELLE: I should have known better.

ARTHUR: My leg! My leg!

ISABELLE: Get out! Mr. Bretagne! Leave my brother alone! *A few seconds more of tugging at* BRETAGNE, *while* ARTHUR *moans from pain.*

BRETAGNE: *suddenly comes to himself. Is immediately quite formal, as his only defense.* Oh, Arthur. I'm sorry. Truly, I'm sorry.

ARTHUR: Just — go.

BRETAGNE: I shall write Verlaine to tell him you are still alive. Goodbye. *He shakily nods to the women and leaves.*

The New York Transit Authority

JOSEPH LAZARUS

THE NEW YORK TRANSIT AUTHORITY was seen at the Playwrights Workshop Club, 14 Cooper Square, New York City, in April, 1972. The production was directed by Craig Barish and featured the following actors:

DELMORE	Frederick Bailey
LINDA (a model)	Arlene Alexander
BRENDA (an old lady)	Pat Lazarus
RABBI	Dov Gottesseld
PREGNANT WOMAN	Mary Jane Creamer
LOUIS (a fashion designer)	Wally Duquet
MOTORMAN	Nick Discenza
POLICEMAN	Joe Lo Grippa
VOICE OF GOD	Robert Barger

Other production: Theatre 77 Rep, June, 1973, directed by Rod Clavery.

Synopsis: Six passengers on a stalled subway train engage in conversation, each slowly revealing the focus of his or her life. It soon becomes apparent that the events occurring on this train—such as a motorman who burns incense—are somewhat extraordinary. LOUIS, who has been drinking, leans out an open door to throw up, and is horrified to find that the train is "suspended in space." The doors shut and the train begins to move.

DELMORE: *checks his watch.* Eleven A.M.

RABBI: *checks his.* No.

LOUIE: *checks his.* Fellas, it's 9 P.M.

BRENDA: *checks hers.* Three o'clock in the afternoon. You're all drunk.

PREGNANT WOMAN: *checking hers.* I don't want to say this . . .

LINDA: *checking hers.* Don't.

DELMORE: Louis. You're sober now?

LOUIE: Yes.

DELMORE: I don't know why I believe you. But you look sober.

LOUIE: Yes.

DELMORE: You're going to Atlantic Avenue, Brooklyn? From Manhattan?

LOUIE: Yes? Yes.

DELMORE: And I'm going from Brooklyn Heights to the West Bronx. And he's going to Union Square? And she's going to Long Island?

BRENDA: Flushing.

DELMORE: That's impossible.

LOUIE: That's right.

DELMORE: And . . .

LOUIE: We're hanging in space.

LINDA: Moving backwards.

PREGNANT WOMAN: Moving. Moving. *Groans.*

DELMORE: I followed the ...

LOUIE: Red line!

LINDA: The sign!

RABBI: Same station sign!

DELMORE: ... blue line!

PREGNANT WOMAN *groans.*

BRENDA: Now I don't know what I did.

DELMORE: It is pretty goddamn plain to see that something fishy is going on here, wherever that is, now, whatever that is, and it is not my fault, nor is it yours. I'm not accusing anyone in particular, because no one in particular is ever to blame in these situations, but this time someone or some group has gone too far. Just a wee bit too far. For years I've put up with much quietly. I've asked myself, "What can you do, individually, Delmore Rosenblatt?" The answer, of course, is "nothing." But I see now that I've been asking the wrong question. I should have asked, "What can you do, collectively, Delmore Rosenblatt?" I never asked this question because I had enough problems at home and at work. I never thought to ask it because I'm a person with a keen sense of responsibility. But I ask it now to me and to all of you. And the answer is plain. MUTINY!

BRENDA: What?

DELMORE: Get back at the sons of bitches! MUTINY!

BRENDA: I'm with you pal. *Takes out a cigarette and lights it. As* BRENDA *lights up, the* POLICEMAN *and* MOTORMAN *enter.*

DELMORE: *strikes a Judo pose.* Hah!

MOTORMAN: What is goin' on here? Have you all gone crazy?

PATROLMAN: It looks like a . . . what do you call that thing?

MOTORMAN: Mutiny?

DELMORE: *charges.* Eeeyii!

LINDA: Don't . . .

MOTORMAN *grabs* DELMORE *and pins his arms.*

PATROLMAN: *slugs* DELMORE. No, that wasn't the word.

MOTORMAN: *kicks* DELMORE *as he falls.* Rebellion?

LOUIE: No! No!

PATROLMAN: *slugs* DELMORE *again.* No, that wasn't the word. Mess. They all look like a mess. Yeah. You! *He rips the cigarette out of* BRENDA*'s mouth.* You shouldn't do that! *Stamps on it.*

MOTORMAN: *like she's nuts.* That could mean a fifty dollar fine, lady!

PATROLMAN: *pointing to* PREGNANT WOMAN. What's the matter with her? PREGNANT WOMAN *whimpers.*

MOTORMAN: *kindly.* Why don't you answer the man, mam?

PREGNANT WOMAN: He'll yell at me.

MOTORMAN: Oh, no. Talk to him. You must remember the pressure he's been under.

PATROLMAN: I've been very nervous lately.

MOTORMAN: But he means well. It's just that certain conditions have changed and its' all very difficult to cope with.

PATROLMAN: Yeah.

PREGNANT WOMAN: I'm sorry. *Soft moan.*

PATROLMAN: Anything bothering you?

PREGNANT WOMAN: Oh, no, I'm fine.

PATROLMAN: You're sure?

PREGNANT WOMAN: *to herself . . . The people around her freeze.* Stop pain. No way. No way. The whole world very . . . very . . buttons, sewing machines, very close world, vacuum cleaners, T.V., dizzy, very dizzy, hyperventilation, damned breathing exercises, moving, oh no, pain go away. What will Dr. La Maze say? Naughty Norma. Naughty. Naughty. Oh . . . Fuck you, Dr. La Maze. No, no, that's not what they're trying to teach me. Do not frighten yourself. Think of what's in store, Norma, think of your motherhood, the joys. Be natural. Concentrate. Relax. The joys: mops, pails, detergents, rubber, plastic, much plastic, plastic mops, pails, dishes, baby toys, a plastic basinet. The rainbow colored basinet which won't match any room in the place. Oh, joy to the plastic basinet. Thanks, sister-in-law, for such a crumby gift. Oh, my Donald, where did you find such a sister with such lousy taste, or an Aunt Helen who tells such crude stories, or a mother who wants to name our baby? Where did you get your family, Donald? Oh no, stop, oh, Donald, you're supposed to be here holding my hand with that god-damned Dr. La Maze. We're all supposed to gather in a circle and tell each other how much we want this stinking kid. Donald, it's your fault that I'm having this baby now in this hellhole. No one can blame these people around here or the subway system or anyone except you. You bear the ultimate responsibility!

The Women's Representative

SUN YU

THE WOMEN'S REPRESENTATIVE was seen at the Night House, 249 West 18th Street, New York City, in May, 1973. It was adapted by David Gaard, directed by Pamela DeSio, and featured the following actors:

MRS. WANG	Dolores Kenan
TSUI-LAN	Lisa Shreve
WANG KUEI-YUNG	Linda Kampley
AUNT NIU	Roberta Pikser
WANG CHIANG	Dempster Leech

Synopsis: While CHIANG, *a farmer in a rural Chinese village, has been away on an extended trip, his wife,* KUEI, *has become the Women's Repreesntative—organizing the village women for "spare-time work and learning to read and write."* CHIANG *returns to find his infant son being cared for by his mother,* MRS. WANG, *while* KUEI *is out performing her official duties. He leaves in a rage to find her;* KUEI *returns and takes the baby from* MRS. WANG.

CHIANG *bursts into the room. His right trouser leg is torn.* KUEI *puts the baby on the kang and rushes to him, bending down to examine his leg.*

KUEI: I hope you haven't scratched your leg. *Standing.* Sit down on the kang. I'll mend it for you.

CHIANG: *immobile.* Get away from me!

KUEI: What's the matter? Why are you acting like this the minute you come home?

CHIANG: Like what? It's a hell of a lot better than the way you're acting! What made you finally come back?

KUEI: Why shouldn't I come back? This is my home, isn't it? Haven't you come home too? Have you eaten?

MRS. WANG: He has eaten. Why could you not come home earlier to attend to him?

KUEI: *starting toward outer door.* I'll boil you some water to drink.

CHIANG: *blocking her way.* Don't be so kind-hearted! What did I tell you before I left? You were to stay home and look after the house. A woman shouldn't be going around getting mixed up in all sorts of things. But you paid no attention.

KUEI: I only organized the women for spare-time work and learning to read and write. You don't expect me to stick in the house all day, do you?

MRS. WANG: Hush child! "Men may roam the country, but women should only travel round the stove." The old sayings are right. That is why Chiang is angry.

KUEI: *going to* MRS. WANG. I can't travel around the stove all the time! When I've finished the household chores, why can't I go and do some studying?

CHIANG: *shouting.* Suppose you don't study, then what?

KUEI: *rushing to the baby and picking him up.* Don't scare the baby.

MRS. WANG: *snatching the baby from* KUEI-YUNG. Even if the Yangtse floods and is filled with turbulence, must our home be such also? Remember the baby. He is not offending anyone. Why should he suffer with you? *Takes baby into inner room.*

CHIANG: Now you listen to me. Starting from today, you're going to stay home. Unless I say so, don't you dare think of going anywhere. In my house, there will be no hens crowing at dawn or mares becoming battle-chargers.

KUEI: You can stop trying to bring back the old set of rules. Today is today! I'm not a pig to be shut up in a sty whenever you give the word. If you try to trample me underfoot again, I'm not going to take it!

CHIANG: *approaching her menacingly.* Why, you dirty, shameless wench!

KUEI: *earnestly.* How have I behaved shamelessly? I walk straight and do what is right. What have I done for you to call me shameless?

CHIANG: Damn you, how dare you answer me back? I'll teach you a lesson, you see if I don't! *Looks wildly for something to hit her with, sees nothing and dashes out outer door.* KUEI-YUNG *quickly bolts door.* CHIANG *shouts and pounds the doors.* MRS. WANG *hurries in from the inner room.* KUEI-YUNG *runs to her.*

MRS. WANG: What holocaust is descending upon our family?

CHIANG: *off stage.* Open up, open up I say!

KUEI: He wants to beat me.

MRS. WANG: You have offended him.

KUEI: I have offended him / I have offended him? Who has offended whom? He's being unreasonable!

CHIANG: *off stage.* I'll show you who I am! Open up, open up this minute! *Furiously pounding the door.*

KUEI: Don't break the door down. I'll open it. *Goes to door and is about to open it.*

MRS. WANG: *rushing to* KUEI-YUNG *and pulling her back to other side of the room.* He'll have a stick in his hand. He is liable to smash things.

The door breaks and CHIANG *bursts into the middle of the room holding a whip.* MRS. WANG *stands between him and* KUEI-YUNG.

MRS. WANG: Stop! Your minds have been heard from as well as your hearts. She has yielded to her husband. What good will this now do?

CHIANG: Who says she's yielded to my wishes? I say one word and she answers back with ten!

MRS. WANG: She may not say so, but in her heart she has yielded to you. She sees you as master of her house and respects you as such. She will not go against your wishes. *Taking whip from* CHIANG. Come now, give that thing to me. *Going to* KUEI-YUNG. The best swimmers are always the ones who get drowned, and the best talkers are the ones that get beaten. I was a young wife myself once. Do what he tells you. *Sitting on kang.* In marriage ask not who is correct but what is correct.

CHIANG: You don't think men like me let themselves be run by their women, do you? I told you one thing and you did exactly the opposite. I told you to stay away from that women's association, but you had to take the lead in all their trouble-making! Did you think I wasn't coming back?

KUIEI: You're back now, but that doesn't mean you can do everything without any help. A man can't block out the sky with one hand. Ask anybody—is it a crime to attend literacy class and do women's welfare work? I haven't done badly with the work either. I not only sew and cook, I did the ploughing and weeding too!

MRS. WANG: Tut, tut, Kuei-Yung. You ploughed and weeded because you wanted to. Your husband didn't force you, and neither did I. But a woman is a woman. Ploughing and weeding is a man's job. Only peasant women go into the fields.

CHIANG: Stop wasting words on her. *To* KUEI. You'd better get this straight. Don't think you can put on airs just because you gave a hand in the fields. That doesn't mean a thing to me. From now on you're not to do it! And I want you to resign from the women's association and the youth league. If I catch you running around again, I'll break your legs!

KUEI: You wouldn't dare!

CHIANG: You'll see if I dare. Just try gadding about again.

MRS. WANG: *leaving whip on kang, rising.* Daughter-in-law! Hold your tongue. My life has passed with enough event without this. *To* CHIANG. You have been away working for three months. You have returned to your home at last. It is time we all rest; the day has been long and many things have happened. Your quarrel is finished. Now let the patterns of our lives again flow smoothly. She can not remain the women's representative forever. "To admit defeat is to allow the heart to bleed." Let us all go to bed. *To* KUEI. A husband's temper is as necessary to a good home as the kettle of rice on the stove. Do not argue any more. It is getting late, time for bed.

MRS. WANG: *standing near chest.* He would like his padded ones. Where are they?

KUEI *takes slippers from drawer in chest and places them on the floor before* CHIANG.

KUEI: Would you like to wash your feet?

CHIANG: Yes!

KUEI *goes to outer room.*

MRS. WANG: *going to kang and picking up whip.* Scare her only, that is all that is needed to make her behave. But do not hit her!

CHIANG: If I don't act a little tough with her, she'll be even harder to handle in the future.

MRS. WANG: I am afraid you can not do anything just by force. Have you not heard there is a Marriage Law now? The government does not allow men to beat their wives any longer. They have instituted something they call "divorce."

CHIANG: She must obey the man who feeds her. I'm not going to pamper her.

MRS. WANG: We are a respected family. Do not make a scene. It will cause the neighbors to laugh at us. KUEI *enters.*

KUEI: The basin is waiting for you in the next room. CHIANG *goes out.*

MRS. WANG: *taking whip with her and picking up* CHIANG'*s shoes.* Do not sit up and waste lamp oil. Go to bed. *Goes off to inner room.* KUEI *removes her scarf and puts it in the chest.* CHIANG *enters.*

CHIANG: Damn it, a nice pair of pants ruined all because of you, you jinx. *Sits on kang.*

KUEI: Why do you treat me like this the minute you get back? What have I done wrong?

CHIANG: Don't play innocent with me! Did you obey any of my orders?

KUEI: But maybe your orders weren't quite right. I'm leading the handicraft group, but after all, I also earned extra income for the family. I've learned a little in the literacy class and it will come in handy. We're already using new farm implements, and the time is coming when we'll be using tractors. How will we work then, if we cant' even read or write? Just look around. Everyone is studying, everyone is trying to improve. *Kneels besides him on the kang.*

CHIANG: That's got nothing to do with you! Just because you can scribble a few lousy words is no reason for you to go around making a fool of yourself. I suppose our home isn't good enough for you!

KUEI: How have I been making a fool of myself? You've only just come back. Why don't you find out what I've really been doing before you say things like that?

CHIANG: I've found out all I want to know. I saw through you long ago!

MRS. WANG *comes from inner room, goes to pick up two quilts from quilt pile and begins laying them out on the kang, shooing them off it.*

MRS. WANG: Time to go to bed! In the silence of the night, even the tormented vultures find peace!

KUEI: Don't you bother, Ma. I'll do it soon.

MRS. WANG: No, I'll do it. *Continues making bed.* KUEI *helps her.*

Young people move very slowly when there is important work to be done, only the old know how few tomorrows there are in which to be happy.

CHIANG: Don't make the bed for her. Why should you serve her?

MRS. WANG: Please. When trouble disorders our lives, it becomes sorrow.

CHIANG: I'm not going to let you! *Grabs quilts and throws them to the floor.*

MRS. WANG: *picking up quilts.* You are a grown man. Do not let the child in you remind us of someone who left us long ago. *Laying out bed again.* It is time we all rested. A little quarrel between husband and wife should cause no more excitement than a little rain in spring.

Mrs. Peacock

STANLEY NELSON

MRS. PEACOCK was seen at Theatre 77 Rep, 23 East 20th Street, New York City, in October, 1973. The production was directed by Shelly Desai and featured the following actors:

MRS. PEACOCK	Marin Riley
MISS SALTINO	Judith Hink
DITCHIK	Al Amateau
FLORA	Joan Durr
ALAN	Dick Sisk
SAFFRON	Fred Versacci

Other production: Omni Theatre Club, July, 1970, directed by Viktor Allen.

Synopsis: MRS. PEACOCK, *a resident of Old Folks Home who whiles away much of her time in rambling soliloquies, has become quite exercised about a stuck window in her room. To calm her down,* MISS SALTINO, *a rather sadistic nurse, has injected a sedative into her rump.* FLORA, *her daughter, comes for a visit.*

In MRS. PEACOCK's *room. As the lights come up,* FLORA *is sitting by the edge of the bed, shaking her mother.*

FLORA: Mother . . . Mother!

MRS. PEACOCK: *half asleep.* What . . . what is it? *Opens eyes.* Oh, it's you, Flora. I had hoped it might be someone exciting.

FLORA: *ignoring her remark.* I just happened to be in the neighborhood, mother. I thought it would be nice to drop in and chat.

MRS. PEACOCK: Yes, it's nice, it's terribly nice that you come to visit me once or twice a month.

FLORA: *firmly.* You know that isn't true. Look, let's not run through those tasteless clichés about all children being ingrates and forgetting the sacrifices, okay? Besides, you never made any sacrifices.

MRS. PEACOCK: No?

FLORA: No. And if my visits are as infrequent as you say, you should feel compelled to make them as pleasant as possible so that we can both enjoy them.

MRS. PEACOCK: Buried somewhere in those remarks, I suppose, is an irreducible logic.

FLORA: Of course. *She lights a cigarette.*

MRS. PEACOCK: You're not supposed to smoke, Flora.

FLORA: They don't mind.

MRS. PEACOCK: *sighing.* All right. I'll be pleasant. Let's chitter-chatter.

FLORA: *pausing, then almost mechanically.* It was pleasant on the parkway. The sun shone on the carhoods and on the puddles left from yesterday's rain. I made good time.

MRS. PEACOCK: There's a new girl who came in and gave me my massage after lunch. She has soft hands; so soothing. Her hands are never cold. Most hands are cold.

FLORA: Jamie said the cutest thing today. He said: "If I can't be President, then I'd like to be City Manager." I pointed out that it's harder to be City Manager than it is to be President.

MRS. PEACOCK: The food is getting better. Today for dinner, we had mushroom barley soup, fish sticks and custard pie. I didn't eat the custard pie; I never did care for sweets . . .

FLORA: I had my hair done today. *Pause.* Do you like it?

MRS. PEACOCK: Your hair—your hair looks beautiful, Flora.

FLORA: Thank you.

MRS. PEACOCK: *after pause.* You've changed your brand of cigarettes, Flora.

FLORA: *singing.* "A change in the weather, a change in the sea . . ."

MRS. PEACOCK: Why?

FLORA: Why?

MRS. PEACOCK: Why did you change your brand of cigarettes, Flora?

FLORA: Oh—I don't know. I get bored. So do countless other people. So they try a new brand of cigarettes.

MRS. PEACOCK: Is the filter recessed, Flora?

FLORA: Sure. I don't want to get throat cancer.

MRS. PEACOCK: No one in our family ever had throat cancer, Flora. We're diabetic, as a rule.

FLORA: Diabetic? I didn't know that.

MRS. PEACOCK: Better get a checkup, Flora. *Pause.* I'm tired of this chitter-chatter. *Pause.* Why don't you leave?

FLORA: Please don't get testy again. Why should I leave? I just arrived.

MRS. PEACOCK: All right, daughter. Then stay. But for heaven's sake, let's stop this chitter-chattering. For once in our lives, let's talk about something important.

FLORA: *uncomfortable*. You mean like . . . civil rights . . . Cambodia?

MRS. PEACOCK: To hell with Cambodia! That's not important!

FLORA: *annoyed*. Then *you* tell *me* what's important.

MRS. PEACOCK: I'll tell you what's important. Death. Death. Death is important. Your death is important. My death is important.

FLORA: But our people are dying in Cambodia.

MRS. PEACOCK: To hell with them! They can worry about their own deaths. I must worry about my death.

FLORA: But people don't brood about such things, Mother. They make provisions, and that's that.

MRS. PEACOCK: I have provided for you, Flora.

FLORA: Mother, I wasn't. . . .

MRS. PEACOCK: I know you weren't, Flora. But now we've gotten that out of the way, and we can talk about my death. How will I die, Flora? How will it be?

FLORA: Mother, people just don't speak about this anymore. They just don't speak about it this way; it's old-fashioned, obsolete.

MRS. PEACOCK: That's what they say about life. That's how they live.

FLORA: *agitated*. There you go again with that abstract *they*. Who is *they*? What is *they*?

MRS. PEACOCK: Are you going to fight with me, Flora? Just because I flushed your turtle down the drain? Can't you ever forgive me?

FLORA: *regaining control.* You're becoming disconnected, Mother. Just because you're aging. . . .

MRS. PEACOCK: Aging? I'm not aging . . . I'm aged. *Raising her voice.* I'm putrefying in this bed like a character from Edgar Allan Poe!

FLORA: Please keep your voice down, Mother. They told me at Welfare ———

MRS. PEACOCK: Welfare? Stop treating me like a child! Don't you think I know that Welfare is a myth dreamed up by you and Miss Saltino? Don't you think I know that Miss Saltino calls me Mrs. Pigeon just to be sadistic? *Her voice becomes even louder.* Don't you think I know that Miss Saltino listens in on my soliloquies about being painfully ill and that I put on these performances just for her benefit?

MISS SALTINO: *entering left.* I'm afraid your time is up, Mrs. Binghampton.

FLORA: *relieved, stands.* Yes, thank you. Goodbye, Mother. *She kisses* MRS. PEACOCK'S *forehead and exits quickly.*

MRS. PEACOCK: *calling after her daughter.* Don't let them put tubes in me, Flora! Don't let them syphon off my pus and my blood and my guts! I have a right to die! I want to . . . MISS SALTINO *again jabs the needle into* MRS. PEACOCK'S *arm.* C'est la vie . . . every hour on the hour . . . no news is good news. . . .

Applejuice

FRANCINE TREVENS

APPLEJUICE was seen at the Joseph Jefferson Theatre, 11 East 29th Street, New York City, in August, 1973. The production was directed by Emelise Aleandri and featured the following actors:

LEE COOPERMAN	Joan Abrahams
NAGLE	William T. Jones
EVELYN AND OTHERS	Joan Nelson
MOVIE STAR, OTHERS	Emelise Aleandri
ADAM AND OTHERS	Jeff McLaughlin
THE DEVIL, ALBERT, OTHERS	Bob Tennenhouse

Synopsis: APPLEJUICE *is a revue about, among other things, Adam and Eve, women's lib, male-female relations and the textile industry. Below are two scenes from the play.*

Lights up on painter at easel, woman posing in chair with severe black wig.

LEONARDO: At last, your portrait, she is finished, Madame Gioconda.

LA GIOCONDA: Ah, now may I see it? *Rises to approach.*

LEONARDO: No, no, no, no—not until you tell me WHAT made you smile like-a that.

LA GIOCONDA: *with that smile.* I have a secret!!

LEONARDO: Unless you share it with me, I shall never show you your portrait. *She pouts.* That smile, it haunts, it plagues, people will wonder forever—what made that smile?

LA GIOCONDA: You did, Maestro.

LEONARDO: On you face, not on my canvas.

LA GIOCONDA: Again, you did.

LEONARDO: *ripping off his smock ardently.* You were smiling that way at ME?

LA GIOCONDA: Not precisely. Your maid, Mona and my servant girl, Lisa, they are sisters. On Mona's day off, she visits Lisa at my villa . . .

LEONARDO: Mona—Lisa—what have they to do with this portrait?

LA GIOCONDA: Mona tells Lisa all the secrets of her master, Leonardo De Vinci and I, in my boudoir, hear all. *That smile.* Naughty, naughty . . . you have the big clay feet, Maestro!

LEONARDO: You know all my secrets?

LA GIOCONDA: *nodding, with that smile.* By name and title.

LEONARDO: *tossing his arms up in the air dramatically.* Madre Mia!

LA GIOCONDA: Oh! *puts her hand to her mouth a moment, then lowers it slowly to reveal that smile.* I didn't know about your MOTHER!!!

BLACKOUT

Lights up on reporter with long scroll and woman with curled, powdered wig.

REPORTER: How does it feel to be the mother of the country, Mrs. WashingTIN?

MARTHA: Washing*ton* as in weight, not TIN as in ear.

REPORTER: Yes, well, pardon me . . .

MARTHA: That's all right, as long as you spell it correctly in the papers!! Being Mother of the Country is rather too many children for me, at my age. I was never the mother type.

REPORTER: You must be mighty proud of what your husband did, Mrs. Washingtin-ton!

MARTHA: *wearily*. What's he done now? His name's always getting in the papers, and my family always felt the only time to be in the papers is when you get born, married, or died. He didn't DIE did he?

REPORTER: No, no, pardon me if I gave that impression, but—I mean about his becoming President.

MARTHA: Oh, THAT! Personally, I thought that was a bit of all right. But crossing the Delaware, in midwinter . . .! I told him that was sheer heroics!

REPORTER: For what do you think history will remember the President?

MARTHA: About ten or twenty years, I expect.

REPORTER: No, I meant, when you think of your husband while he is away, what do you think about most?

MARTHA *hesitates, ponders, running her tongue through her cheek.* How restful it is not hearing those wooden false teeth of his cloppety clop in my ear.

REPORTER: FALSE teeth? *The next is said in shock, full face front.* Something false about the President!!! *He takes a moment to recover.* Pardon me, Madam, but don't you realize what a hero your husband is to the country?

MARTHA: I've heard. Frankly, now that I've matured, I prefer the intellectual type. *She pats her hair.* Take Ben Franklin. Old Benjy, now there's a man. *She giggles like a girl.* Of course, he did invent those teeth for George . . . But good old Ben Franklin doesn't wear them. He opens his mouth, you get pearls of wisdom, not wooden pearly whites . . .

BENJAMIN: Hey, Marty—wanna come play with my lighting rod?

MARTHA: Oh, pardon me!! *Hands teacup to reporter.*

REPORTER: But Mrs. Washington . . .?

MARTHA: *giggling as she hugs Benjamin.* I have a little experimenting to do.

REPORTER *drinks tea for blackout.*

222 Off-Off Broadway Theatres

EDITOR'S NOTE: *All theatres and addresses off-off Broadway are subject to fluctuation. Some may be out of business by the time this guide appears. Productions are often staged on a highly irregular basis. All theatres listed are located in Manhattan, unless otherwise indicated.*

1. Abbey Theatre, 136 East 13th Street, 598-2401
2. Academy Arts Theatre Company, 100 Seventh Avenue
3. ACSTA, 251 West 80th Street, PL 5-5120
4. Actors & Directors Alliance, 321 W. 74th Street
5. Actor's Experimental Unit, 682 6th Avenue, JU 2-4240
6. Actor's Mobile Theatre, 156 West 72nd Street, 877-9140
7. Actor's Place at St. Luke's, 487 Hudson Street, 663-5047
8. Actor's Playhouse, 100 Seventh Avenue
9. Actor's Studio, 432 West 44th Street, PL 7-0870
10. Afro-American Singing Theatre, No Permanent Theatre, 222-8487
11. Afro-American Theatre, 415 West 127th Street, 866-2389
12. Afro-American Total Theatre, 33 Riverside Drive (Suite 16E), 799-3290
13. Airline Theatre Wing, Madison Avenue Baptist Church, 31st Street & Madison Avenue, MU 5-1377
14. Alamo Playwrights Unit, 218 West 48th Street
15. All Souls Players, Unitarian Church of All Souls, Lexington Avenue at 80th Street, LA 5-5530
16. Amas Repertory Theatre, 4 West 76th Street, 873-3207
17. AMDA Theatre, 150 Bleeker Street, 677-5400
18. American Ensemble Company, No Permanent Theatre, Box 5478 Grand Central Station, 938-1608
19. American Mime Theatre, 192 Third Avenue, SP 7-1710

OFF-OFF THEATRES

20. American Noh Theatre, No Permanent Theatre, 42 Ave. of Americas
21. American Place Theatre, 423 West 46th Street, 246-3730
22. American Stanislavski Center, 139 West 13th Street, PL 5-5120
23. American Theatre Company, 106 East 14th Street, 989-0023
24. American Theatre Lab, 219 West 19th Street, 691-6500
25. Arena Repertory VII, 277 Park Avenue South, 673-9430
26. Association of Theatre Artists, YM-YMHA, Washington Heights —Inwood, 569-6200
27. Bed-Stuy Theatre, 1407 Bedford Avenue, Brooklyn, N.Y. 636-9700
28. Bel Canto Opera, East 31st Street
29. Black Vibrations, No Permanent Theatre, 778-4878
30. Blackfriars Guild, 316 West 57th Street, CI 7-0236
31. Blue Dome, 261 Bowery, 437-9829
32. The Brooklyn Company, 144 7th Avenue, Brooklyn, N.Y.
33. Brownsville Theatre Lab, 338 Riverdale Avenue, Brooklyn, 342-9519
34. Cabaret Theatre at Noon, St. Peter's Gate, 16 East 56th Street. PL 3-4669
35. Campbell Hall, 455 West 51st Street, CI-5-7264
36. Central Arts, 108 E. 64th Street, PL 8-6327
37. Chelsea Theatre, Brooklyn Academy, 30 Lafayette Street, Brooklyn, N.Y., 783-6700
38. Chichi/Castenango, 189 Second Avenue, 581-6470
39. Church of the Good Shepard, 240 East 31st Street, 982-3202
40. Church of the Covenant, 310 East 42nd Street
41. Church of the Holy Communion, 6th Avenue and 20th Street, CH 3-5262
42. Circle Theatre, 2307 Broadway, 874-1080
43. Clark Center for Performing Arts, 840 8th Ave., 246-4818
44. Community Loft, 106th Street & Broadway
45. Compania of Teatro Repertorio Espanol, 138 E. 27th Street, 889-2850

46. The Company, Holy Family Auditorium, 315 East 47th Street, 753-3425
47. The Cornbread Players (Billie Holiday Theatre), 1368-90 Fulton Street, Brooklyn, N.Y., 636-0918
48. Courtyard Playhouse, 137A West 14th Street, 424 West 48th Street, 741-1180
49. CSC Repertory Theatre, Abbey Theatre, 136 E. 13th Street, 677-4210
50. Cubiculo Theatre, 414 West 51st Street, 265-2138
51. Ron Dener Workshop & Undercroft Theatre, 240 East 31st Street, 689-1519
52. Demi-Gods, 344 West 36th Street, 924-4671.
53. Direct Theatre, 401 E. 81st Street, 737-2366
54. Donnell Library Center Auditorium, 20 West 53rd Street, 790-6463
55. Dove Theatre Company, 346 West 20th Street, WA 9-2390
56. Down Stage Studio Theatre, 321 West 14th Street
57. Dramatis Personae, 114 West 14th Street, 675-9922
58. Dr. Quackenburgh's Traveling Medicine Show, 427 West 59th Street, 245-9656
59. Dume Spanish Theatre, 409 West 44th Street, 765-3457
60. Duo Theatre Workshop, 522 East 12th Street
61. Drama Tree Players, 182 5th Avenue, AL 5-6353
62. Drifting Traffic, 520 La Guardia Place, Sandra Shurin, 673-2802
63. The East River Players, 237 East 104 Street, LE 4-7900
64. East Village Theatre, 433 East 6th Street
65. Eastern Opera Theatre of New York, 530 E. 89th St., 744-5035
66. Elbee Audio Players, 621 West End Avenue, TR 4-5704
67. Encore Studio, 2345 64th Street, Brooklyn, N.Y.
68. Equity Library Theatre, 310 Riverside Drive, 663-2028
69. Expression of Two Arts Theatre, 102 West 29th Street, PE 6-5668
70. Flatbush Dutch Reform Church, Flatbush & Church Ave.,

OFF-OFF THEATRES

      Brooklyn, N.Y. 693-5296
71. Focus II, 163 West 74th Street, 362-9188
      956-4774
72. Fordham University at Lincoln Center, 113 W. 60th Street,
73. Fortune Theatre, 62 East 4th Street, 473-9698
74. Friday Theatre, 241½ East 84th Street
75. Fulton Theatre Company, 441 West 26th Street, 524-6700
76. The Gallery Players, 186 St. Johns Place, Brooklyn, N.Y., 622-1037
77. Gilberto Zaldivar's Spanish Theatre Repertory Company, 138 East 37th Street, 889-2850
78. Gracie Square Theatre, 334 East 79th Street
79. Grand Theatre, 70 Grand Street, 431-5446
80. 98 Greene Street Loft, 98 Greene Street, 966-7673
81. Greenwich House, 27 Barrow Street, 242-4140
82. Guild Studio I, Ansonia Hotel, Broadway & 73rd Street
83. Hamm & Clov Stage Company, 89 West 3rd Street, 477-5770
84. Harbor East Players, St. John's Church, Webster Avenue & Ocean Parkway, Brooklyn, N.Y.
85. Harlem Little Theatre, 180 West 125th Street
86. Heights Players, 26 Willow Place, Brooklyn, N.Y., 237-2752
87. Henry Street Playhouse, 466 Grand Street, WO 2-1100
88. Henry Street Settlement's New Federal Theatre, 240 East 3rd St., 674-1414
89. Hotel Bretton Hall, 2350 Broadway, SU 7-7000
90. Hudson Guild Theatre, 441 West 26th Street, 524-6700
91. Ice and Fire Theatre Company, 23 St. Marks Place, 473-8933
92. Iglesias' Theatre Club, 178 Houston Street, 260-1872, CH 3-9268
93. Immanuel Theatre, 88 Street & Lexington Avenue
94. Innercourt Theatre, 504 Grand Street
95. The Intense Family, Traveling Theatre, 799-4970
96. Interart Theatre, 549 W. 52nd Street, 246-6569
97. International Arts Relations, 508 West 53rd Street, 582-9875

98. Jean Cocteau Theatre, 43 Bond Street, 765-1300
99. Joseph Jefferson Theatre Company, 1 East 29th Street, 288-0900
100. Judson Poets Theatre, 55 Washington Square South, 777-0033
101. Kings Players, 118 8th Avenue, Brooklyn; 275 Clinton, 638-5766
102. Knickerbocker Creative Theatre Foundation, No Permanent Theatre
103. Kuku Ryku Theatre Lab, 147 Spring Street, 966-1365
104. Lambs Club Theatre, 128 West 44th Street, JU 2-1515
105. Levy-Shea, 100 East 16th Street, 677-5690
106. Library of Performing Arts, Lincoln Center, 799-2200
107. Light Opera Company of Manhattan, Jan Hus Theatre 351 East 74 Street, 535-6310
108. Lolly's Theatre Club, 808 Lexington Avenue, 832-7404
109. Malachy Company, Traveling Company, 237 E. 62nd St., TR 7-9434
110. La Mama Experimental Theatre, 74A East 4th Street, 474-7710
111. Manhardt Theatre Foundation, 542 La Guardia Place
112. Mama Hare's Tree Company, 13 Street Theatre, 741-2796
113. Manhattan Project Theatre Company, NYU School of Arts, 111 Second Avenue, 598-7678
114. Manhattan Theatre Club, 321 East 73rd Street, 288-2500
115. The Mask, 125 Fifth Avenue
116. Master Opera, 310 Riverside Drive, 733-2204
117. Master Workslab Theatre, 152 Remsen Street, Brooklyn, N.Y., 982-7510
118. Matrix Players, All Angels Church, 262 West 81st St., 724-9271
119. The Medals Company, Josephine Baird Home, 340 West 55th Street, 582-3320
120. Memorial Presbyterian Church, 186 St. Johns Place & 7th Ave., Brooklyn, N.Y., NE 8-5541
121. Meri-Mini Players, 4 West 76th Street
122. Mixed Doubles Company, Broadway & 86th St., 874-4758
123. Mongoose Community Center, 782 Union Street, Brooklyn, N.Y., 783-8819

OFF-OFF THEATRES

124. Mt. Olivet Church, 86 Street & West 12th Street, Brooklyn, N.Y. HI 9-2663
125. Music Theatre Lab, 490 Riverside Drive, RI 9-7000 ext. 124
126. National Arts Club, 15 Gramercy Park, GR 5-3424
127. National Black Theatre, 9 East 125th Street, 534-9882
128. Negro Ensemble Company, 133 2nd Avenue, 674-3530
129. New Heritage Repertory Theatre, Inc. 43 East 125 St., 876-3272
130. New Lafayette Theatre, 2349 7th Avenue, 862-2460
131. New Repertory Company, 455 W. 43rd St., 489-1816
132. New Village Theatre, 433 East 6th Street, 475-9506
133. New York Arts Theatre, 25 East 4th St., 228-1338
134. New York League of Playwrights, 162 West 21st Street
135. New York Lyric Opera Company, 124 W. 72nd St., Donald Johnston, TR 4-1993
136. New York Shakespeare Festival, 425 Lafayette St. & Lincoln Center, 677-1750
137. New York Theatre of the Americas, 427 West 59th St., 245-9656
138. New York Theatre Ensemble, 62 East 4th St., 254-5913
139. Night House, 249 West 18th Street, 691-7359
140. Nodeldinis Park East, 1311 Madison Avenue, 722-9489
141. Nuestro Theatre, 108 West End Avenue, 873-4113
142. Omni Theatre Club, 145 West 18th Street, LT 1-6470
143. Ontological-Hysteric Theatre, 80 Wooster St., 260-3328
144. Open Theatre, 423 West 46th Street, CI 6-7277
145. Opera Buffa Company, 316 E. 88th Street
146. Opposites Company, 141 Prince Street
147. Other Theatre, 351 Riverside Drive, 666-8440
148. Pageant Players, 450 Broome Street
149. Park Avenue Community Theatre, 593 Park Avenue & 63rd Street, TE 8-0808
150. Park Slope Cultural Center, 186 St. Johns Place, Brooklyn, N.Y., 622-1037
151. Peach Pits, 200 West 24th Street, 242-3900
152. The Peoples Performing Company, 59 Carmine St., 243-1373

153. Performance Group, 33 Wooster Street, 691-5434
154. Playbox, 94 St. Marks Place, 243-1373
155. Players Workshop, 81 East 4th Street, 677-3540
156. Playwright's Foundation Theatre, 124 Bank Street
157. Playwright's Unit, 83 East 4th Street
158. Playwright's Workshop Club (Bastiano's) 23 St. Marks, 473-8933
159. Potbelly Theatre Workshop, 40 West 18th Street
160. The Pretenders Theatre, 106 East 16th Street
161. Primitive Theatre, 33 Howard Street, 966-2155
162. Public Theatre, 425 Lafayette St., 677-6350
163. Quarry Theatre Corp., 441 West End Ave., 362-4863.
164. Repertory VII, 427 West 59th Street, 245-9656
165. The Ridiculous Theatre Company, 50 West 13th Street, 924-9785, 691-5434
166. Riverside Church Theatre, 490 Riverside Drive, 749-8140
167. Riverside Theatre Workshop, St. Johns-in-the-Village, 218 West 11th Street, 666-7170
168. Root Theatre, 74 Trinity Place, 425-6677
169. Roundabout Theatre, 307 West 26th Street, 924-7161
170. Royal Playhouse, 219 2nd Avenue, GR 5-9647
171. Saint Clements Theatre, 423 West 46th Street, CI 6-7277
172. Saint George's Church, 135-32 28 Ave., Flushing, N.Y., 371-1540
173. Saint Peter's Gate, St. Peter's Lutheran Church, 16 East 56th Street, 758-5843
174. Samuel Rubin Theatre, 35 5th Avenue
175. Schreiber Studio, 386 3rd Avenue, 874-7509
176. Section Ten, 8 Waverly Place, 598-3429
177. Senior Dramatic Workshop, 154 West 57th Street, JU 6-4800
178. Seventy Four Below Coffee House, 74 Trinity Place, 269-6640 Ext. 298
179. Shade Company, 230 Canal Street, 431-3479
180. Shaliko Company, No Permanent Theatre, 40 E. 7th St., 598-2401

OFF-OFF THEATRES

181. South Bronx Community Theatre
182. South Street Seaport Theatre-On-The-Pier, 16 Fulton St., 265-5597
183. Space for Innovative Development, 344 West 36th St., 947-4671
184. Spencer Memorial Church, 152 Remsen Street, Brooklyn, N.Y.
185. Splinters Company Foundation, Inc., 52 Greenwich Ave., 924-1422
186. Stage 73, 321 East 73 Street, 595-5222
187. Stagelights Theatre Club, 218 West 48th Street, 265-8344
188. Stagelights Two, 125 West 22nd Street, 989-9228
189. Teatro Arena, 277 Park Avenue South, 362-0330
190. Ten Penny Players, 709 Greenwich Street
191. Terrain Gallery, 39 Grove Street, WA 4-4984
192. Theatre Asylum, 33 Wooster St., 691-2220
193. Theatre Black, Traveling Theatre, 647-6245
194. Teatro Caras Nuevas, 114 West 14th Street
195. Theatre Forum, 333 6th Ave. at 4th Street, 4th Floor, 586-4800
196. Theatre Genesis, St. Mark's Place Church In-The-Bowery, 2nd Avenue and 10th Street, 533-4650
197. Theatre of Latin America Inc., 321 E. 73rd St. 628-2814
198. Theatre of Madness at the Bank, 1 Front Street, Brooklyn, N.Y. 855-6419
199. Theatre for the New City, 113 Jane Street, 691-2220
200. Theatre Projects Company, 161 West 22nd Street, LT 1-6470
201. Teatro do Orilla, 214 East 2nd Street, 260-2548
202. Theatre 77 Repertory, 23 East 20th Street, JU 2-4240
203. Theatre Three, Sloane House, 356 West 34th Street, OX 5-5133
204. Theatre Unlimited, 171 West 85th Street, 799-2886
205. Thirteenth Street, 50 West 13th Street, WA 9-4336
206. TPG, 548 La Guardia Place
207. Triangle Theatre, Holy Trinity Church, 316 East 88th St. AT 9-4100
208. Trinity Church, Broadway & Wall Street
209. Truck and Warehouse Theatre, 79 East 4th Street, 677-8330
210. Universalist Church, 76 Street & Central Park West, 675-7230

211. University Streets, 130 East 7th Street
212. Upstage at Jimmy's, 33 West 52nd Street, 757-8484
213. Urban Arts Corp., Church of Holy Communion, 26 West 20 Street, 924-7820
214. Venture Theatre Club, 232 8th Avenue, 924-1348
215. Voices Inc., Mt. Morris Park Amphitheatre, 122 Street & Morris Park West, 663-3100
216. Washington Square Methodist Church, 133 West 4th Street, SP 7-2528
217. Westbeth Playwrights Feminist Collective, 463 West Street, 691-0015
218. West Side Community Repertory Theatre, 252 West 81st Street, 874-9400
219. The Weusi Kumba Theatre, 393 Dumont Avenue, Brooklyn, N.Y. HY 6-4593
220. Women's Interart Center, 549 West 52nd Street, 246-6570
221. WPA, 333 Bowery, 473-9345
222. Zarattini's Free Academy, 47 Bond Street, 777-5171